PREACHERS

WHO MADE A

DIFFERENCE

Preachers
who made a difference

Peter Jeffery

EVANGELICAL PRESS

EVANGELICAL PRESS
Faverdale North Industrial Estate, Darlington, DL3 0PH, England

Evangelical Press USA
P. O. Box 825, Webster, New York 14580, USA

e-mail: sales@evangelicalpress.org

web: http://www.evangelicalpress.org

First published 2004

British Library Cataloguing in Publication Data available

ISBN 0 85234 5755

Printed and bound in the USA

6037091

Preachers
who made a difference

Even if you are not a preacher, this is a book that will fire you up. It will introduce you to the lives of nine very different men who opened the Bible, preached Christ and saw people changed forever. You will learn about their strengths, weaknesses and struggles. You will have a small taste of their sermons — especially if you also listen to the accompanying CD. You will come to understand what true preaching is and will long for its return today. Best of all, you will find that your heart has often been moved to pray to the only one who can raise up such preachers as these.

Stuart Olyott
Pastoral Director of the Evangelical Movement of Wales

Contents

Introduction

Preaching should confront men and women with God and eternity. In order to do this it has to be biblical. It has to tell people what God is saying in his Word. From the preacher's point of view this does two things. It helps to give him an authority that is far more than his own ability and gifts of oratory. People need to know that God is speaking through his servant. Secondly, it gives the preacher an endless source of material to preach. He is not dependent upon current events for his sermon topics, but has a huge reservoir of biblical teaching to draw upon.

The men we are looking at in this book were Bible-men. They varied in nationality, temperament and sometimes in doctrine but they all sought to bring God to the people. This is why they made a difference. They set out not merely to inform people but to transform them. The most drastic and radical transformation that a man can know is that from spiritual death to spiritual life. These men preached for this. They knew that the sinner's greatest need is for regeneration so they preached to reach his heart and soul. This governed how they communi-

cated and created in them a great desire to preach Christ, the
cross and his redeeming blood.

They preached to create a conviction of sin in the unbe-
liever. It is not conviction of sin for a man to feel bad because
he is drinking too much or generally making a mess of his life.
Sin is not just a violation of socially accepted standards. To see
sin only in social or moral terms will not lead people to conviction. Sin must be seen in the light of the law and holiness of
God. The gospel is not an aspirin for the aches of life, to soothe
and comfort man in his misery. It is a holy God's answer to the
violation of divine law by human beings whose very nature is to
rebel against him.

Most people think salvation is the product of morality and
religious observance. In spite of the clarity of the New Testament message, they still cling to their own efforts to save themselves. But salvation by works never creates conviction of sin
because it fails miserably to take into account the holiness,
purity and justice of God. It sees sin only as a moral or social
blemish and not as an affront to the Word, law and character of
God. It is the law of God which produces conviction because it
shows us our sin in relationship, not to society and people, but
to God. It shows us that we have failed to meet God's require-
ments.

A common feature of all great preachers is a longing for
success — to see souls saved. Andrew Bonar says of Robert
Murray M'Cheyne, 'He entertained so full a persuasion that a
faithful minister has every reason to expect to see souls converted under him, that when this was withheld, he began to fear
that some hidden evil was provoking the Lord and grieving the
Spirit. And ought it not to be so with all of us? Ought we not to
suspect, either that we are not living near to God, or that our
message is not a true transcript of the glad tidings, in both
matter and manner, when we see no souls brought to Jesus?'[1]

Bonar continues, 'Two things he seems never to have ceased from — the cultivation of personal holiness and the most anxious efforts to win souls.'[2] How M'Cheyne links these two things is highly significant. He wrote to William Burns in September 1840, 'I am also deepened in my conviction, that if we are to be instruments in such a work, we must be purified from all filthiness of the flesh and spirit. Oh, cry for personal holiness, constant nearness to God, by the blood of the Lamb. Bask in his beams — lie back in the arms of love — be filled with his Spirit — or all success in the ministry will only be to your own everlasting confusion... How much more useful might we be, if we were only more free from pride, self conceit, personal vanity, or some secret sin that our heart knows. Oh! hateful sins, that destroy our peace and ruin souls.'[3]

M'Cheyne believed that 'In the case of a faithful ministry, success is the rule and the lack of it the exception.'[4] And when there was no success, no souls saved, he did not blame the people but looked first at his own heart.

Born not made

Preachers are born not made. Was Jeremiah the only preacher set apart by God before he was born? (Jeremiah 1:5). Was he an exception or the norm? Preachers are not the products of education and training but are men set apart by God and equipped by the Holy Spirit for their life's work. This does not mean that they do not need training, but above all there needs to be the call of God. Neither Spurgeon or Lloyd-Jones had formal theological training but it was obvious that they were prepared by God and that his hand was upon them. Preaching is a special gift from God and those who have it need to guard it carefully and seek to nurture it for use to God's glory.

Many evangelicals today have lost confidence in preaching. We may lament this and mourn the fact that in some churches music and drama have replaced preaching. But why has it happened? Is it not the fault of preachers themselves? Is it not because gospel preaching too often lacks authority, relevance and power, and consequently fails to save souls? It has been said that the most urgent need in the Christian church today is true preaching. Most preachers would agree with that but many Christians in the pew do not. That is not surprising if the preaching they hear is so sentimental as to have no substance, or so intellectual that they cannot understand it.

What constitutes true gospel preaching? It involves both a proper content and a correct presentation. The gospel must be preached in a language that people can understand. In the last century Spurgeon was pleading, 'We need in the ministry, now and in all time, men of plain speech. The preacher' s language must not be that of the classroom, but of all classes; not of the university, but of the universe... "use market language", said George Whitefield, and we know the result. We need men who not only speak so that they can be understood, but so that they cannot be misunderstood.'[5] Plain speech is not slang but simple language and concepts that people can understand.

Preachers will only make a difference when their preaching clearly shows the people the Lord Jesus Christ. The only difference that is of any significance is the one Christ makes in the hearts of men and women. It is possible for a preacher to make a difference to his hearers that is only temporary. He comes and preaches and makes a great impact but if you passed that way in a year's time you would see that there is now no longer any difference to be seen. It was only temporary and this is because it was not the gospel, not Christ, that made the difference but the preacher himself. Such preaching is only a form of entertainment. It does not confront sinners with God but merely holds their attention for a while until something else comes along.

A serious responsibility

Preaching is not a hobby but should occupy a man's whole life and thinking. The preacher sees everything in relationship to his ministry. In this sense he is never on holiday. His mind is continuously taken up with the next sermon and the next congregation. The seriousness of the matter causes what Paul calls in 1 Corinthians 2:3-4 a 'trembling'. What do we know of this trembling? Why did Paul with all his great abilities preach in weakness, fear and trembling? Surely it must have been because he felt the awesome responsibility preaching puts upon a man.

Preachers who make a difference know something of this trembling. It was said of M'Cheyne that when he entered the pulpit people would weep before he opened his mouth — to quote Lloyd-Jones, 'There was something about his face, and in the conviction which his hearers possessed that he had come from God; he was already preaching before he opened his mouth. A man sent from God is aware of this burden. He trembles because of the momentous consequences, the issues, that depend upon what he does.'[6]

Preaching is the most exciting and uncertain activity a man can partake in. The preacher never knows what is going to happen when he steps into a pulpit. In fact, anything can happen when the power of the Holy Spirit comes and divine unction dominates the ministry. Thomas Olivers was antagonistic to the gospel and went to hear George Whitefield preach in the open air with the intention of disrupting the meeting. But when the preacher started he was unable to interrupt and was compelled to listen. Whitefield had a bad turn in his eye and his enemies called him Dr Squintum, but Olivers said that it did not matter which way Whitefield's head was facing, 'his eye was always on me.' He was saved and went on to write that great hymn 'The God of Abraham Praise'.

Preaching is also a battle because the devil hates it. He does not mind men who get into a pulpit to give a nice, gentle homily, but he hates it when Christ is uplifted and sinners are confronted with the holy God. This battle takes many forms. Sometimes it is in the heart and mind of the preacher as he grapples with his own unworthiness. Sometimes the devil attacks him before he leaves home for church with tensions with his children. Sometimes the attack is frontal. One of the greatest preachers I have ever heard was the late Douglas MacMillan of Scotland. Douglas was preaching for us in Rugby at a series of evangelistic meetings. I was ill in bed and unable to attend. After the service Douglas came into my bedroom to see me and I could see by his face that the service had not gone well.

Some of the young men of the church had gone into the streets to try to get passers-by to come in. They persuaded two twelve-year-old boys to come. The boys came in and were quiet throughout the service but Douglas told me that he felt evil coming from one of these boys which bound him in his preaching. Douglas MacMillan was a strong man physically, intellectually and spiritually, yet this twelve year old boy so affected his preaching that he felt bound. That has to be the attack of Satan.

Preaching is no cosy chat but a taking on of hell in preaching the gospel to sinners. The best of sermons can be left flat and lifeless. The greatest sense of expectancy can be dashed. But the opposite is also true, and such power can come from God onto the preaching that is inexplicable in terms of anything merely human. Heaven and hell lock in battle when the gospel is preached.

Unction

Great preachers are so only because God is pleased to bless their preaching and use them in remarkable ways. They will have other things going for them, such as natural abilities, but it is God who makes the difference. They are aware of this and are continuously sensitive to the hand of God on them. To them this is the only thing that matters. They will prepare their sermons diligently and seek to prepare themselves spiritually, but they do not depend on these and all the time they look for divine unction.

Dr. Lloyd-Jones once told a minister's conference, 'You think my sermons come down from heaven each Saturday evening on a silver plate, but they don't. I have to work for them.' The Doctor was stressing the need for careful preparation of the sermon, but he also knew that there was more needed. He said,

> Seek Him! Seek Him! What can we do without Him? Seek Him! Seek Him always. But go beyond seeking Him; expect Him. Do you expect anything to happen when you get up to preach in a pulpit? Or do you just say to yourself, 'Well, I have prepared my address, I am going to give them this address; some of them will appreciate it and some will not. Are you expecting it to be the turning point in someone's life? Are you expecting anyone to have a climactic experience? That is what preaching is meant to do. That is what you find in the Bible and in the subsequent history of the Church. Seek this power, expect this power, yearn for this power; and when the power comes, yield to Him. Do not resist. Forget all about your sermon if necessary. Let Him loose you, let Him manifest His power in you and through you. I am certain, as I have said several times before, that nothing

but a return of this power of the Spirit on our preaching is
going to avail us anything. This makes true preaching,
and it is the greatest need of all today — never more so.
Nothing can substitute for this. But, given this, you will
have a people who will be anxious and ready to be
taught and instructed, and led ever further and more
deeply into 'the Truth as it is in Christ Jesus'. This 'unction', this 'anointing', is the supreme thing. Seek it until
you have it; be content with nothing less. Go on until you
can say, 'And my speech and my preaching was not with
enticing words of man's wisdom, but in demonstration of
the Spirit and of power.' He is still able to do 'exceeding
abundantly above all that we can ask or think.'[7]

The preacher needs God with him in the pulpit. He not only
preaches about God but he wants also to experience the
presence of God with him as he preaches. If he does not he will
cease to make a difference. He may continue to be popular and
to a degree be useful, but he will not be making the difference
that matters.

References

[1] A. Bonar. *Memoirs & Remains*, Middleton, 1965, p.79.

[2] Bonar, p.150.

[3] Bonar, p.250.

[4] Bonar, p.250.

[5] C. H. Spurgeon, Banner of Truth Trust Magazine, April 1960.

[6] M. Lloyd-Jones, *Knowing the Times*. Banner of Truth Trust, 1989,
p.325.

[7] M. Lloyd-Jones, *Preaching & Preachers*. Zondervan, 1972, p.325.

1.

Hugh Latimer

Latimer was born in 1485 near Lutterworth in Leicestershire. This was the town where 100 years previously the great reformer John Wycliffe had preached. However, there could have been no greater difference in beliefs between Wycliffe and Latimer. Latimer regarded the teaching of Scripture to be heresy and sought to oppose all such activities. In fact when he gained his Bachelor of Divinity he chose to speak before the whole university at Cambridge on 'Philip Melancthon and his doctrines'. He attempted to expose the dangers of reformed doctrine and the congregation at Great St. Mary's Church received his sermon extremely well.

One man who listened, but not with agreement, was Thomas Bilney. As he listened God gave Bilney a burden to see Hugh Latimer saved and the student prayed for an opportunity to speak to this champion of Roman Catholicism. Douglas Wood tells us how this prayer was answered;

Shortly after his sermon in front of the university, Latimer heard a knock on his study door. When he opened it, there stood Bilney. Latimer was astonished. What could he want? 'For the love of God, be pleased to hear my confession', Bilney pleaded.

Latimer was astounded. The heretic wanted to make confession to the Catholic. He felt a sense of triumph.

'My sermon has converted him,' Latimer thought. 'If he returns to the church, the others will soon follow suit!'

He eagerly agreed to the request. Bilney knelt before him and he waited for the expected confession of disobedience to the church, of reading and teaching others false doctrine, and so leading them astray from the path marked out by their spiritual fathers. Instead, Bilney recounted how he had bought pardons, paid for masses and gone on pilgrimages, but all to no avail. He told Latimer of the anguish he had suffered in his soul and the uselessness of everything that the church had prescribed. He then spoke of the peace that had come to him after he had bought Erasmus's New Testament and read in its pages that Jesus Christ is the Lamb of God that takes away the sin of the world.

At first Latimer listened without mistrust — he had heard countless confessions from penitents — but as Bilney continued he became disturbed. He had expected penitence, but this was nothing but a confession of faith. He wanted to get away from Bilney, yet something in the latter's quiet simplicity commanded his attention.

At length the sovereign grace of God prevailed in Latimer's heart. Like Paul, he had been fighting against God but now he was conquered and, like the apostle, his conversion was instantaneous...[1]

Latimer must have learnt many valuable lessons in the circumstances of his conversion that would benefit his preaching in later years. Bilney's determination that he should hear the gospel would undoubtedly fortify him in circumstances he would have to face later in his ministry. A preacher without this passion for souls is not of much use to God. Also Bilney's confidence in the truth of the gospel was inspiring. True, he had to resort to an unusual method to get Latimer to hear, but it was the message of Christ and his salvation that he faithfully conveyed. Sometimes the more conventional methods of preaching are closed to us, but this should not stop the desire to see souls saved. There are always ways and means to share the gospel with sinners, and a preacher must be alert to the best way in given circumstances to reach the lost with the truth.

Ingenuity for the sake of it is not to be commended, but ingenuity when all other doors are closed is both to be commended and imitated.

Preaching

Latimer was saved. He bought a New Testament to read for himself and found help and encouragement in study with Bilney and other reformers at Cambridge. His conversion took place in 1524 and he was soon using his energy and eloquence to preach. D'Aubigne said, 'What Tyndale was to be for England by his writings, Latimer was to be by his discourses.'[2] He preached in Latin to the clergy and in English to the people. Whoever he addressed, Latimer's words were always fearless and uncompromising even when challenging prelates, most of which he considered to be more busy with their own self interest than the eternal salvation of their flocks[3]

His gospel preaching was just as clear and addressed very much to the times he lived in. He said one day:

If one man had committed all the sins since Adam, you may be sure he should be punished with the same horror of death, in such a sort as all men in the world should have suffered... Such was the pain Christ endured... If our Saviour had committed all the sins of the world; all that I for my part have done, all that you for your part have done, and that any man else hath done; if He had done all this himself, His agony that He suffered should have been no greater nor grievous than it was... Believe in Jesus Christ, and you shall overcome death... 'But, alas!' said he at another time, 'the devil, by the help of that Italian bishop yonder, his chaplain, has laboured by all means that he might frustrate the death of Christ and the merits of his passion.'[4]

The Lord blessed such preaching and many were converted. Latimer tells us of one convert who 'was a popish woman, and savoured not of Jesus Christ. In process (of time) she tasted that the Lord is gracious. She had such a savour, such a sweetness and feeling that she thought it long to the day of execution. She was with Christ already, as touching faith, longing depart and to be with Him. The Word of God had so wrought in her'.[5]

Opposition

Such preaching as Latimer's would inevitably arouse opposition from the church authorities and Nicholas West, Bishop of Ely, suspended his licence to preach. Latimer was now in the same position Bilney had been in. The desire was there to make Christ known, but with all pulpits closed to him what was he to do? When men close doors, God will always have means of opening them.

Robert Barnes, an Augustine monk was prior to the abbey at Cambridge and the bishop's ban did not cover the abbey, so Barnes opened his pulpit to Latimer. Further to this Cardinal

Wolsey gave Latimer his licence to preach so all pulpits in England, including Cambridge, were now opened to the reformer.

This was an unsettled time in England, however as matters of state mingled with the need for church reformation. King Henry VIII's desire for Anne Boleyn ultimately led him to seek a divorce from his wife Catherine of Aragon. When the pope forbade this, Wolsey (as the angry king's first minister) was condemned and died on November 30th 1530 on his way to be tried for treason.

Dealings with the king

By 1530 Latimer had been noticed by the most powerful in the land, and he was placed on the Cambridge commission to examine the question of the king's marriage. This enabled Latimer to win the esteem of Henry's deputy, Doctor Butts, the court physician, who had presented him to his master, by whose orders he preached at Windsor.'[6]

The king heard about this and decided that Latimer could be of some help to him in his desire for a divorce. In March 1530 Latimer preached before the king for the first time and continued to preach at court throughout Lent. He was then invited to be part of a commission the king set up to examine which religious books circulating in England were good, and which should be banned. Douglas Wood says,

> Latimer could see clearly that the church had set up its voice in place of Christ's, but no Reformer could agree to this. The people must have the Bible to read for themselves to hear the voice of Christ.
>
> Unfortunately Latimer and his friends were completely outnumbered. Tyndale's works were condemned as 'full

of great errors and pestilent heresies', his New Testament translation and also the Pentateuch, which was now complete, were both heavily censured and their use banned. What must have seemed the crowning insult to Latimer was the fact that his name was 'appended' with the others of the commission to a proclamation that he had opposed and which he hated with all his heart.[7]

Wood continues,

True to type, Latimer did not let matters rest there. After much thought, he sat down and wrote a letter to Henry later that year in which he asked that there might be free circulation of the Holy Scriptures in English. Henry made a promise and however vague it was; Latimer grasped it firmly since it was the only hope for England. Together with the other Reformers, he knew that there could be no reform or progress unless the Word of God had free course. His one hope was that Henry's conscience would be stirred. It was a noble letter and a bold one. Latimer knew full well that people who addressed Henry boldly normally had a short life but that did not deter him.

The letter is too long to quote in full but this portion gives us a good idea of what it was like. 'You have promised us the Word of God, perform your promise now rather than tomorrow,' Latimer wrote. 'God will have the faith defended, not by man or man's power, but by His Word only, by the which He hath evermore defended it, and that by a way far above man's power or reason, as all the stories of the Bible make mention… The day is at hand when you shall give an account of your office, and of the blood that hath been shed with your sword.' Latimer risked his life by using this language but he was prepared for death if need be.[8]

Our days are not Latimer's and the dangers of upsetting the powers that be are not so drastic, but there are still dangers. Preachers are not to be concerned if their sermons upset the leaders of the church. Their life will not be at stake but their living maybe, and this can put them under pressure to water down the message. No preacher is immune to this and at some point and to some degree, Latimer's courage and faithfulness to the Scriptures ought to encourage them and keep them steadfast in their preaching. It is God we are to please not men.

Persecution

Latimer moved in 1531 to West Kington in Wiltshire where he became Rector. He was glad to be away from the politics and intrigue of court, but a man like Latimer would never be far away from controversy. It was not that his temperament was contentious and caused difficulties, but rather the doctrines he preached. In 16th century England biblical Christianity was a rarity and biblical principles unknown even to bishops and priests.

Men either loved or hated the preaching of Hugh Latimer. There is no hatred like that of those who hate Scripture, and this hatred inevitably spills over to those who preach the Bible. This was brought home harshly to Latimer in 1531 when Thomas Bilney was burnt at the stake at Norwich. D'Aubigne says, 'One martyrdom was not sufficient for the enemies of the Reformation. Stokesley, Lee, Gardiner, and other prelates and priests, feeling themselves guilty towards Rome, which they had sacrificed to their personal ambition, desired to expiate their faults by sacrificing the reformers. Seeing at their feet a fatal gulf, dug between them and the Roman pontiff by their faithlessness, they desired to fill it up with corpses. The persecution continued.'[9]

Latimer was a prime target for the persecution and he was commanded to appear before Bishop Stokesley. After weeks of trial he was persuaded to meet his enemies half way. Douglas Wood asks, why did Latimer change like this?

From adamant refusal, he appears to have suddenly weakened. The strong-minded yeoman's son, who was prepared to face a king and stand for the truth, seems to have crumbled and become weaker than Bilney. But physically he was less robust and in his letter to Warham he tells how his health had deteriorated: 'My head is so out of frame, and my whole body so weak.' In his letters during that winter and spring he continually complained of pains in the head. Apart from the constant interrogation, his state of health goes a long way to explain — while it does not excuse — his sudden change and submission.[10]

Meanwhile Henry divorced Catherine and married Anne Boleyn. Cranmer was now Archbishop of Canterbury and the Reformation in England was growing stronger. Although Henry's divorce had instigated the break with Rome, the Reformation was not based on this, but on the doctrines preached by men like Bilney, Cranmer and Latimer, and particularly the work of William Tyndale in translating the Scriptures into English. Anne Boleyn was also a warm supporter of making the New Testament available to the people.

In 1535 Latimer was appointed Bishop of Worcester. D'Aubigne says the appointment was largely due to the influence of the Queen. 'Anne Boleyn was so charmed by his evangelical simplicity, Christian eloquence, and apostolic zeal, that shortly she used her influence with the king to have the preacher elevated to the see of Worcester. Latimer takes his place by the side of Cranmer among the reformers of the English Church.'[11]

Henry VIII broke with Rome in order to attain his divorce but he was never a Protestant let alone a Christian. He remained in belief and action a Roman Catholic. Still, in 1538 he made it law for a copy of the Bible in English to be placed in every church in England. In contradiction to this he was willing to persecute those who held Protestant doctrine. It seems Henry used Catholicism and Protestantism as he willed in order to promote his own ends.

Henry's daughter Elizabeth was like her father, but his two other children, Edward and Mary, held extremely strong beliefs. Edward was only young but he held firm Protestant sympathies, whilst Mary Tudor was a passionate Catholic. These were volatile years for the reformers — the godly Edward succeeded Henry in 1547 when he was only nine years but died in 1553 and Mary came to the throne. Immediately severe persecution of Protestants began and Hugh Latimer was among those who died by being burnt at the stake.

Last years

Latimer resigned as Bishop of Worcester in July 1539. Whether the resignation was demanded by Henry or freely made by Latimer is not clear, but what is clear is that Latimer was delighted. He said, 'Now I am rid of a heavy burden and never did my shoulders feel so light.' From then until Henry's death his ministry was limited and obscure. When Edward came to the throne Latimer began to preach again. Wood says,

> Latimer did the work of an evangelist and his years of si
> lence had given a depth and maturity to his preaching
> that made him the greatest preacher of his day, a man

who could reach the hearts of all classes of English people. Wherever Latimer preached, large crowds gathered to listen. His quaint but animated eloquence made a deep impression on the hearts and minds of his hearers. When he was called to preach before the court, a pulpit had to be erected in the king's garden in order to provide enough space for the crowd that thronged to hear him. Later, when he preached in St Margaret's Church, Westminster, the people crushed in and broke the pews. Latimer was regarded as the apostle of the English Reformation and all recognised that he was not only the ruthless enemy of the superstitions and heresies of Rome, but also a stern preacher against the social vices and sins of his age.[12]

Mary Tudor was proclaimed Queen on July 19th 1533 and on September 13th of the same year Latimer was brought before the Privy Council and for his 'seditious demeanour,' was locked up in the Tower of London. Archbishop Cranmer and Bishop Ridley were imprisoned at the same time. On October 16th 1555 Latimer and Ridley were burnt at Oxford.

Latimer's words to Ridley as they were tied to the stakes sums up his faith and character, 'Be of good comfort, Master Ridley, and play the man. We shall this day light such a candle, by God's grace in England, as I trust shall never be put out.'[13]

Please refer to Track 1 of the accompanying CD. Extracts from a sermon preached by Hugh Latimer at St. Paul's Cross in January 1548.

References

[1] D. Wood, *Such a Candle,* Evangelical Press, 1980, pp.8-10.

[2] D'Aubigne, *The Reformation in England,* Vol 1, Banner of Truth Trust, 1962, p.207.

[3] D'Aubigne, *Reformation,* p.206.

[4] D'Aubigne, *Reformation,* p.207.

[5] D'Aubigne, *Reformation,* p.208.

[6] D'Aubigne, *Reformation,* p.458.

[7] Wood, *Candle,* p.43.

[8] Wood, *Candle,* p.44.

[9] D'Aubigne, *Reformation,* Vol 2, p.76.

[10] Wood, *Candle,* p.62.

[11] D'Aubigne, *Reformation,* Vol 2, p.183.

[12] Wood, *Candle,* p.147.

[13] Wood, *Candle,* p.168.

2.

John Knox

John Knox was not a gentle and humble sort of man who everyone could love and respect. On the contrary, he was fiery, passionate and aggressive. When he was born Scotland was thoroughly Roman Catholic. Over the years reformers had come along and nibbled at the Catholicism of the land. Knox was no nibbler. He took Rome on headfirst and shattered its control of Scottish life. This did not make him popular and this unpopularity continues still.

It is not surprising that Knox has been unpopular. Mark Galli said,

> Knox could be arrogant, proud, stubborn, and cantankerous. He called Catholic Queen Mary of England, to put it in modern parlance, "A freak of nature." Of course, tact is not a gift usually lavished on a prophet, which is the best way to understand Knox. He was a Hebrew Jeremiah set down on Scottish soil — in a relentless campaign of fiery oratory, he sought to destroy idolatry and purify national religion. In the end, his cause triumphed.[1]

Knox was aware of his reputation and towards the end of his life wrote, 'I know that many have complained much and loudly, and do still complain of my great severity, but God knows that my mind was always free from hatred to the persons of those against whom I denounced the heavy judgements of God.'[2]

It was not that he believed himself to be better than others. On the contrary, he was deeply aware of his own sin. In a letter to his mother-in-law in June 1553 he wrote,

> Although I never lack the presence and plain image of my own wretched infirmity, yet seeing sin so manifestly abounds in all estates, I am compelled to thunder out the threatenings of God against the obstinate rebels ... Judge not, mother, that I write these things, debasing myself otherwise than I am — no, I am worse than my pen can express ... there is no vice repugning to God's holy will expressed in his law, wherewith my heart is not infected.[3]

The sort of ministry to which God called John Knox was never going to make him popular. It is easy to criticise him but he was a man of his day. The demands and challenges of the 16th century were vastly different from our own, so it is not possible to judge him by modern standards. Popular or not, no one could question the enormous difference Knox made to the religious life of his nation. It was a difference that changed the history of Scotland for centuries.

Early years

Although the date of Knox's birth is uncertain and dates given vary between 1505 and 1514, historians today believe that

the latter of those dates is most likely. He had a good education and was ordained a priest in April 1536. In 1543 he was
greatly influenced by the preaching of a converted friar
named Thomas Guilliame. Tudur Jones says that this
preaching made a Protestant of Knox.[4]

Knox's call to Christian ministry is of interest to anyone
considering this direction themselves. Initially Knox was
extremely reluctant to preach; indeed following the call of
his congregation in 1547 he was so overcome the gravity of
the charge that he burst into tears then spent the next few
days alone. As Thomas M'Crie noted in 1811, this reverent
attitude was in stark contrast to the conduct of many of the
grasping priests of the time and indeed, it serves to remind
us today of the awesome responsibility of proclaiming the
gospel.[5]

John Knox was not one to tone down his views to gain
approval and was drawn into controversy with Catholicism
straight away. His first public sermon for example, followed
an open debate with Dean John Annand, a long term
opponent of the reformers. Annand could not defend his
views with Biblical texts, but was instead forced to lean on
the authority of the church for support, a body which had
branded all reformers heretical. For his part, John Knox
asserted that the authority and practices of the Roman
church were unscriptural with such power that the crowd
urged him to preach the following week.

It seems then, that the hesitancy Knox felt regarding his
adequacy for the ministry was conquered by the great need
he saw for more reformers to declare the truth to the people. This will doubtless be a source of encouragement to
those feeling inadequate today — the need to share the
gospel of Jesus with lost people is surely as pressing as in
Knox's day.

Knox chose Daniel 7:24-25 as the text for his first sermon, which was delivered in the public preaching place of St Andrews where he was castle chaplain. He firstly defined the true church and declared God's love for her before detailing the corruptions of the Roman church. Knox courageously proved from the Bible that as justification is by faith alone (Gal. 2:16; 3:11) the works doctrine of Catholicism with its pilgrimages and pardons, must be in direct conflict with the Word of God.

Unsurprisingly, Knox's sermon caused much controversy as there were many canons, friars and the sub-prior present. News soon spread along the church hierarchy resulting in a meeting of reformers and churchmen where the former were challenged to explain their beliefs. Rather than restraining Knox and his colleagues, this gave them another platform to express their views, further reminding us that God works in mysterious ways!

Realising that arguments were not helping their cause, the Catholics then issued orders that only university and abbey preachers should take the parish pulpit on Sundays. To avoid debate, they were warned to avoid speaking on contentious subjects. Knox and his colleagues remained able to speak on weekdays and were delighted that the churchmen would not publicly dispute the reformed stance.

Knox's powerful ministry in St Andrews did not last long; in July of that year the French fleet lay siege to the castle and Knox was captured. Nevertheless, during the few months he was at liberty to preach in the town on weekdays he was greatly used of God and many locals turned to Protestantism. He then spent nineteen months as a galley slave until in 1549, apparently through the intervention of the English Government, 'he was released and his true preaching work began'.[6]

Knox spent the next five years ministering in northern England and then as a royal chaplain to Edward VI until 1553 when the godly young king died. The subsequent rise to power of staunch Catholic Mary Tudor forced Knox into exile in Frankfurt and Geneva where he met John Calvin.

Return to Scotland

On May 2nd 1559 Knox returned to Scotland. Within a year, A. M. Renwick says, 'the Roman Catholic Church had virtually vanished out of the land.'[7] This was no small achievement. The French under Mary of Guise, who had a French army in Edinburgh, ruled Scotland. The Catholics were not going to give up Scotland easily as they viewed it as a base for the destruction of Protestant England.

Two major factors worked towards the cause of Reformation in Scotland. There was the passionate desire in the heart of most Scotsmen to be free from foreign rule. But the greatest force was the preaching of John Knox. Tudur Jones says, 'In the pulpit, he was at his most powerful. He mesmerised thousands of Scots, who were prepared to lay their lives down for Protestantism at his behest. By his preaching, he molded both nobility and ordinary folk into a formidable fighting force and thus left his stamp on the Protestantism of Scotland for centuries to come.'[8]

Mary of Guise died in June 1560, and Mary Queen of Scots arrived in Scotland in August 1561. The previous year the law in Scotland ratified the reformed faith, and Knox was appointed minister of the Church of St. Giles, the great parish church of Edinburgh.

Although the new Catholic Queen promised to support the laws of the land, and to outlaw Mass, she was allowed to continue practising her faith in private. Knox was strongly opposed to this, considering it a foothold for papism in Scotland. Mary soon requested Knox's presence at the palace where she conducted the first of five discussions. He found her to be,

> No mean opponent in argument, and had to acknowl-
> edge the acuteness of her mind, if he could not com-
> mend the qualities of her heart. His attitude from the
> very beginning was unyielding and repelling, abrupt,
> and confrontational, his language and manner harsh
> and uncourt like, perhaps acceptable behaviour for a
> White House news correspondent today, but consid-
> ered rude and disrespectful to a queen in those times. It
> must be remembered that the momentous issues at
> stake required a plainspoken prophet like John the
> Baptist, not a smooth-tongued statesman. Nonetheless
> it might have been wiser at the outset of their inter-
> course, to seek to win rather than repel.[9]

There can be no doubt that Mary wanted to eliminate Protestantism, so she and Knox were never likely to be friends. He knew that the issues at stake were enormous and disputes with the Queen were inevitable. Although, Queen Mary had denied more than once that she intended to sup-press Protestantism and revive Roman Catholicism in Scot-land, history reveals that these denials proved false. Her actions denied her words. She continually withheld financial support from the Protestant ministers and encouraged the celebration of the Mass. John Knox was aware of what was transpiring and remained undaunted, even in the face of much criticism.

Knox preached a sermon on Isaiah 26:13-21 which so infuriated the Queen that she banned him from preaching. This backfired on Mary as the Edinburgh Burgh council backed Knox and issued a statement confirming that '...they will no manner of way consent or grant that his mouth be closit, or he dischargeth of preaching the true Word...[10]

Mary had lost again, but worse was to follow when her husband Lord Darnley was murdered and she ran away with the Earl of Bothwell, who was the suspected murderer. As this outraged both Protestants and Catholics she was forced to abdicate on July 24th 1567.

The preacher

The Reformation in Scotland, as in England, Germany and Switzerland, was essentially a re-recognition of the truth of biblical doctrines and the preaching of those truths. There could have been no reformation anywhere without preaching. J. D. Douglas argues that Knox's preaching was based on four positive principles:

- Holy Scripture is the sole and sufficient rule of faith and practise.
- Man is justified by faith alone.
- The minister is simply teacher of the gospel, servant and steward.
- The people have a voice in electing pastors and office bearers.[11]

Knox's preaching was first of all the proclamation of the good news that God through Jesus Christ saves sinners, saves the ungodly by the gift of the righteousness of his Son, the immaculate Lamb of God. Such preaching will save some and greatly offend others. It has always been this way from the New Testament onwards.

According to Dr Lloyd- Jones,

His great characteristic as a preacher was vehemency. Great preachers are generally vehement; and we should all be vehement. This is not the result of nature only; it arises from the feeling of the power of the gospel. Vehemence is, of course, characterized by power; and John Knox was a most powerful preacher, with the result that he was a most influential preacher. The effect of his preaching upon Edward VI, was quite remarkable; and that was not only true of Edward VI but of many others also. It is traditional to refer to the effect of his preaching on Mary Queen of Scots. He could make her weep; not under conviction but in anger. She was afraid of him; she said she was more afraid of his prayers and his preaching than of many regiments of English soldiers. Randolph, a courtier and an ambassador, said this about him and his preaching: 'The voice of one man is able in one hour to put more life into us than 500 trumpets continually blasting in our ears'. The voice of one man! Many times did one sermon delivered by Knox change the whole situation…That is what preaching can do and has often done. This was constantly the case with Knox.[12]

Please refer to Track 2 of the accompanying CD. Part of a sermon preached by John Knox in August 1565 before the Queen's husband.

References

---

[1] M. Galli, *Christian History*, Vol X1V. No 21, p.6.

[2] Galli, p.17.

[3] Galli, p.17.

[4] Galli, p.9.

[5] T. M'Crie, *The Life of John Knox*, Free Presbyterian Publications, 1991, p.32.

[6] I. Murray, *John Knox*, Evangelical Library Lecture, 1972, p.7.

[7] A. M. Renwick, *The Story of the Church*, IVP, 1958, p.143.

[8] T. Jones, *Christian History*, p.8.

[9] Grace Valley Christian Centre, Lecture notes from 1995 class

[10] L. A. Curto, http://www.reformed.org/*The Watchman of Scotland*, 1990, p.5.

[11] J. D. Douglas, *Great Leaders of the Christian Church*, Moody, p.251.

[12] M. Lloyd-Jones, *The Puritans*, Banner of Truth Trust, 1987, p.266.

3.

Samuel Davies

Dr Martyn Lloyd-Jones speaking to the students of Westminster Theological Seminary, Philadelphia in September 1967 on the subject of preaching said,

> If only we could transport ourselves back two centuries and go down into Philadelphia and listen to George Whitefield, we might learn something about preaching. We would see a master preaching. Then, having listened to Whitefield, if we were fortunate enough, we might listen to Samuel Davies also. You people have neglected Samuel Davies; let me put in a word for him. The greatest preacher you have ever produced in this country was Samuel Davies, the author of the hymn, 'Great God of wonders, all thy ways/Are matchless, godlike, and divine', and the man who followed Jonathan Edwards as president of Princeton. His sermons are still obtainable. Here was another obvious master preacher. At that time, or a few years later, we might have listened to him likewise. If we could only sit and listen to these men, we might know something about preaching.[1]

This is high praise indeed for the preaching of Samuel Davies. Many of his sermons are available in print for us today, though in all probability few Christians will have read them. On the other hand, most Christians will have sung the great hymn written by Davies — 'Great God of Wonders'. The hymn captures something of the richness of his theology and the fervour of his evangelistic concern.

Davies was born in Pennsylvania in 1723 and was converted at the age of fifteen. He was ordained in 1747 and set apart to work as an evangelist among the Presbyterian churches in Virginia who had no pastors. His work centred on Hanover County. He was appalled by the general neglect, and lack of concern about religion. Nevertheless, the preaching of Davies so impressed his listeners that the one month he spent in Hanover had a major impact. When Davies felt compelled to return home because of his health, he took with him a message from the people in Hanover to the Presbytery asking for his permanent services.

Poor health prevented Davies from settling in Hanover until May 1748. This was to be his only pastorate. He remained there until 1759 and two years later he died at the age of 37.

Preacher

Davies's temperament and preaching was ideal for Virginia. Pilcher writes, 'As the champion of moderation and religious toleration in Virginia, Davies did not actively proselyte nor did he enter into a round of name-calling with either his Anglican or his Presbyterian opponents. This is not to say that he did not enjoy entering into a good argument when such was presented. In fact, he occasionally went out of his way to engage in these mental exercises, but he was not impetuous and never abused his opponent with vitriolic language. He attacked arguments rather than individuals, taking great delight in demolishing a chain of reasoning while maintaining a friendly relationship with his adversary, regardless of the difference in their religious beliefs.'[2]

His generosity of spirit was such that he did not care if a man was Presbyterian or Church of England so long as he was saved. Such a warm spirit coupled to a great preaching ability made Samuel Davies a very popular preacher. Iain Murray tells us, 'In a letter dated 23 May 1749 Jonathan Edwards reported to a friend: 'I heard lately a credible account of a remarkable work of conviction and conversion, among whites and negroes, at Hanover, Virginia, under the ministry of Mr Davies, who is lately settled there and has the character of a very ingenious and pious young man.' [3]

Murray notes that within five years of his settlement some five or six hundred people regularly came under Davies ministry in various places. However, Davies' concern for the lost did allow him to grow complacent, 'There were occasions when he journeyed 500 miles in two months, during which time he might preach forty sermons ... Such was the geographical spread of his labours that when a Presbytery was first formed in Virginia in 1755 five ministers served an area that Davies had previously served alone.'[4]

In 1755 of the total population of Virginia of 300,000, about half were black slaves. Often about three hundred gathered to hear Davies preach. He said, '...never have I been so struck with the appearance of an assembly, as when I have glanced my eye to that part of the meetinghouse where they usually sit, adorned, for so it has appeared to me, with so many black countenances eagerly attentive to every word they hear, and frequently bathed in tears. A considerable number, (about an hundred) have been baptised, after a proper time for instruction and having given credible evidence, not only of their acquaintance with the important doctrines of the Christian religion, but also a deep sense of them upon their minds, attested by a life of strict piety and holiness.'[5]

At any time from Laodicia to today, lukewarm religion has been popular, and it was so in 18th century Virginia. Davies preached powerfully against this: 'How common, how fashionable is this lukewarm religion! This is the prevailing epidemical sin of our age and country... We have thousands of Christians, such as they are; as many Christians as white men; but, alas! they are generally of the Laodicean stamp; they are neither hot nor cold. But it is our first concern to know how it is with ourselves; therefore, let this inquiry go round this congregation: Are you not such lukewarm Christians? Is there any fire and life in your devotions? Or are not all your active powers engrossed by other pursuits?'[6]

One visitor to Hanover likened the town under the ministry of Samuel Davies as 'like the suburbs of Heaven'. This bears a rich testimony to the depth and reality of Davies's ministry. There was nothing superficial about his preaching nor about his converts. Grace bit deep into the hearts of his listeners and enriched their lives as nothing else can.

He was always seeking the spiritual health of his congregation and sought to bring Jonathan Edwards to work with him as co-pastor. Pilcher notes that Davies,

> ...gave little thought to personal honours when he invited the famous Edwards to join him, for by so doing he was jeopardising his own position of prestige and leadership in Virginia. Instead, the Virginian's comment on Edwards was that, 'Of all the men I know in America, he appears to me the most fit for this place, I would cheerfully resign him my place.' Edwards had recently been removed from his pulpit at Northampton, Massa-

chusetts, and was admittedly having difficulty finding a new position. 'I am now,' he lamented, 'thrown upon the wide ocean of the world, and know not what will become of me, and my numerous and chargeable family.' Despairing of ever finding a new pulpit in New England, Edwards might have joined Davies in Virginia except that the invitation arrived too late.[7]

The College of New Jersey

The Presbyterian College of New Jersey was opened in May 1747. It settled on a permanent site in Princeton in 1752. Davies was deeply concerned for the success of the college and in 1753 he travelled with Gilbert Tennent to England to raise money for its support.

In February 1757 Aaron Burr the president of the college died, and he was succeeded by Jonathan Edwards, who also died the following year. The trustees then asked the 35 year old Samuel Davies to become president. He had no desire to leave his pastorate at Hanover and declined the invitation. This refusal was strongly supported by his friends in Virginia who wrote,

> The Presbytery readily own, and are deeply sensible of the vast Importance of the College of New Jersey; its present unsettled State, and its Need of a Skilful healing Hand at the Head of it: They are also sensible of Mr. Davies' Influence, Popularity, Moderation, and in many Respects his Literary Accomplishments for so great a Trust. But the Presbytery being best acquainted with the State of Religion in Virginia, and best knowing Mr. Davies' Importance here, can by no means agree to his

Removal, as they foresee Consequences very dangerous to the important Interests of Religion among us;
and therefore cannot deliberately agree so sensibly to
weaken our own Hands, and so deeply wound that
Cause we desire above all things to promote.[8]

Davies had second thoughts about this invitation and
when it was renewed in 1759 he accepted. He was only to
serve the college for eighteen months before his death on
February 4, 1761.

Pilcher says of his life,

That so short a life should have left so rich a legacy is a
phenomenon difficult to appreciate until his accom-
plishments are surveyed — Davies' sermons, in addi-
tion to earning a world-wide reputation for the young
minister during his lifetime, were printed and reprinted
and still used for more than a century after his death;
their content: and organisation provided a source of
instruction for several succeeding generations of
preachers. First of the truly original American hymn
writers, this New Light leader composed works that are
still being sung in some churches in the twentieth century. His poetry, which was widely distributed, distinguished Davies in his own age and, further, was of a
genre profitably studied even today. As pulpit orator,
this Virginia preacher had few peers among his contemporaries either in Great Britain or in America; his
oratory exerted a profound influence on later preachers
and perhaps had a significant effect on Southern secu-
lar oratory of the Revolutionary period. He pioneered
in the education of Negro slaves in Virginia, contributed
measurably to the education of Indians, and came to be

recognised as the foremost educator of his denomination. Finally, as the champion of Virginia Presbyterians and the leading spokesman for religious toleration, Samuel Davies helped lay a firm base for the ultimate separation of church and state in Virginia.[9]

Please refer to Track 3 of the accompanying CD. An extract of a sermon preached by Samuel Davies on John 3:16.

References

[1] M. Lloyd-Jones, *Knowing the Times,* Banner, 1989, pp.262-3.

[2] Pilcher, *Apostle of dissent in colonial Virginia,* University of Tennessee, 1971, p.55.

[3] I. Murray, *Revival & Revivalism,* Banner, 1994, p.9.

[4] Murray, p.9.

[5] Murray, p.12.

[6] Murray, p.11.

[7] Pilcher, p.95.

[8] Pilcher, p.173.

[9] Pilcher, pp.186-7.

4.

John Elias

In the town of Rhuddlan in North Wales in 1802 Sunday had become the great day of the week for sin to run riot. Evil was so rampant in the town that preachers would hardly dare interfere. But one preacher, John Elias, was convinced that God wanted him to preach at Rhuddlan. His friends tried to persuade him otherwise because they knew the danger he would face. Nevertheless he went to Rhuddlan fair in the summer of 1802. John Elias stood on the steps of New Inn, sang Psalm 24 and prayed. The crowd were amazed but remained quiet.

Elias then began to preach from Exodus 34.21 on Sunday observance. This was by all accounts a powerful message. According to Eifion Evans,

His spirit was soon stirred up within him, and the words of the Lord came with amazing force out of his lips, carrying light and conviction home to the consciences and hearts of the wicked. He made some very pertinent ... observations in a powerful manner, suitable to his audience. 'Should we', it was asked, 'rest on the Sabbath day if it were a fine day, the harvest being very wet and bad, and the corn much injured?' 'Yes', he answered in a most powerful tone of voice; 'yes, you should obey the Word of God at *all* times. It is said, "in earing and in harvest thou shalt rest"…

Then he made strong allusions to London and other cities, that were set on fire, which he represented as a punishment from the Lord for the disrespect shown to his holy day. He particularly observed the threatenings in the Word of God for abusing the Sabbath … He also dwelt on the promises made in the Bible to those that keep the day holy.

The people soon became greatly alarmed, appearing as persons guilty and miserable … They seemed panic struck! Indeed, great seriousness and sobriety of mind possessed the multitude! Many were heard saying that they would not on any account go again to such a place to do business on the Sabbath. They kept their word, for such misdeeds were never seen again in Flint-shire. A complete stop was put to the evil so rampant and dreadful at Rhuddlan. This was done, not by any human power, authority, or force, but merely by preaching the gospel.[1]

Sinners were converted through that sermon and Elias was surely right when he said, 'The Lord strengthened me, in the face of a great tumult, to preach at Rhuddlan in a fair held there on a Sunday during the harvest season. He gave me the victory. Very soon the custom was discontinued.'[2]

Every preacher looks for the Lord's strengthening and John Elias knew this on many occasions during his ministry.

The Rhuddlan incident tells us several important things about Elias. He felt deeply when the evil of sin so blatantly challenged the authority of God. He did not live in Rhuddlan so in a sense it was nothing to do with him, but Rhuddlan Fair had become so notorious in North Wales that he believed its challenge to God could not be ignored.

He did not believe there was nothing Christians could do to combat the sin of the world. Rather, he was convinced that preaching the Word of God was enough to oppose all the evils of sin. This belief sprang from a high concept of the power of God and a total trust in preaching as God's means of dealing with sin.

Study

John Elias began preaching in 1794 at the age of twenty. By then he was a converted man and presented himself before his Presbytery at Caernarfon as a candidate for the ministry. He wrote, 'A day to remember, was that one day, — Christmas Day in the year 1794, when I was received a member of the Monthly Meeting, and permission was given me to preach the Gospel of Christ.'[3]

He felt a great need for education. His preaching ability was obvious but he was convinced he needed to learn more in order to make the most of the gift that God had given him. He began to attend the school of Rev. Evan Richards at Caernarfon who said of his pupil, 'John Elias was a fine young man. I would like to see many of the same stamp as he rising again amongst the Methodists. Never had I anyone equal to him for learning. He took in the lesson like a thirsty hart drinking the waters ... But this may be said that the Great King made his tongue only for to preach to the Welsh. He will learn as many as you like of other languages, only he is clumsy in the pronunciation thereof. But as for Welsh, all of us have to yield to him, he is the master of us all.'[4]

Education was important to John Elias and at the age of sixty-seven he said, 'I am still learning, and I see more the need of learning and education every day.'[5]

The time he set aside for study was not a mere academic exercise because a large proportion of that time was spent on his knees. This pattern was to be his for the whole of his ministry. After he had left the room of study his wife would often find his chair sprinkled with tears. One day a tradesman fixed his ladder near the window of Elias's study. As he climbed the ladder to repair the roof he looked into the study and saw the preacher flat on the floor. An hour later, on finishing the work, as he descended the ladder he saw John Elias still in the same position. He was concerned and told a servant what he had seen, she told him not to worry her master was only praying.

Power in preaching is not only a matter of preaching ability, it crucially involves a relationship to God which John Elias so obviously had.

Preaching

John Elias felt desperately the need of the Holy Spirit on his preaching. He wrote in March 1838, a few years before his death,

> Dear brother, my mind is constantly grieved that the divine light and power, once known and felt, do not accompany the ministry in these days ... Few consider the ministry of the Gospel as a means to a high end, and a means only. The best preacher is but an instrument, and the best sermons but means; they will not answer the end, except God himself will work through them. Alas, how few consider that Paul and Apollos are

nothing, and that it is God that does the whole work! O that the day would dawn! O that God would manifest himself! O that the Holy Ghost were on some occasional opportunity so poured under the ministry of some of God's servants, until there should appear an evident difference between his work and everything human, and between the divine ordinances in and through which he works, and those ordinances wherein he hides his face and leaves men to themselves![6]

He had a deep concern that preachers should preach the true gospel. He said, 'There is a great defect in the manner of many preachers. It can scarcely be said that the Gospel is preached by them. Their sermons are very confused; they contain many expressions which are not taught by the Holy Ghost; and subjects are so clothed with new words, that it is difficult to know what is meant. Though these preachers may not be accused of saying what is false, yet, alas, they neglect stating weighty and necessary truths when opportunities offer. By omitting those important portions of truth in their natural connection, the Word is made subservient to subjects never intended. The hearers are led to deny the truth which the preacher leaves out of his sermons. Omitting any truth intentionally in a sermon leads to the denial of it.'[7]

By preaching the gospel, John Elias meant,

It is to declare and publish *good tidings* respecting the way of saving sinners from their sins and the wrath of God, shewing that salvation springs out of the sovereign grace and love of God. *Luke* 21.10, Acts 20.24. *John* 3.16. It is to preach *Christ,* in his person, offices, life, death, resurrection, ascension, and intercession. It is to 'preach Christ crucified'. 1 *Corinthians* 1.23. It is to preach the blessings that are to be received through Christ's merits, reconciliation, forgiveness, justification, sanctification, full salvation. It is to publish Christ as everything which a sinner needs. It is indeed 'the Gospel of our salvation.' 1 *Corinthians* 1.30; *Ephesians* 1.13. It is to invite lost sinners to Christ; to urge them to believe in him, to receive him, and to make use of him. *Acts* 10.36, 43; 16.31. *Romans* 3.22; to.9, 10. It is only by the Gospel that the *Holy Ghost* works savingly on the souls of men. It is the ministration of the Spirit: he works powerfully by it. If we expect him to work on the souls of men, we must preach it purely and fully. *Galatians* 2.5. 2 *Corinthians* 3.8. 1 *Thessalonians* 1.5; 2.13. *Romans* 1.16.[8]

For Elias preaching was never formal or boring, as is evident in a remarkable sermon preached in 1824 against drunkeness. Although a lengthy quotation, the following from Eifion Evans is worth reading as so clearly describes the event;

Are there any drunkards here?' he cried. 'I am afraid there are. I beg of you, will you — at least *today* — control yourselves. If you have no respect for the Almighty, no respect for the laws of your land, no respect for yourselves, will you please — for our sakes today — behave soberly and decently. You are, by attending our meetings and by your drinking and disorderly conduct, undermining our character … We have nothing but our character on which to fall back. We are not rich; we are not learned, we are not gifted, we have no high titles … But we have our character; we have a very high opinion of our character; we are unwilling to allow anybody to destroy our character. But the drunkards who are

attending our Associations are undermining our character. What can we do with them, my brethren?'
Someone made a remark, referring to a sermon that
had been preached that day Elias shook himself. 'I feel
within myself this minute,' he cried, 'to offer them for
sale, by auction, to whomsoever will take them, that
they might not disturb us any more.' Then, at the top of
his voice, with his arm outstretched, as if he held them
in the palm of his hand, he shouted, 'Who will take
them? Who will take them?

Churchmen, will you take them?' 'We? We, in our baptism have professed to renounce the devil and all his
works. No; *we* cannot take them.'

Then, after a moment's silence, 'Independents, will *you*
take them?' 'What? We? We, ages ago, left the Church
of England because of her corruption. No; *we* will not
take them.'

Another interval of silence. 'Baptists, will *you* take
them?' 'We? Certainly not! We dip all our people in
water as a sign that *we* take those who have been
cleansed. No; we will not have them.'

Silence again. 'Wesleyans, will *you* take them?' 'What?
We? Good works is a matter of life with us. We do not
want them.'

Then he stretched forth his arm once again, as if holding the poor drunkards in his hand; and once again, at
the top of his voice he shouted, 'Who will take them?
Who will take them? Who will take them?' Then, suddenly, his whole nature became agitated. His eyes
flashed as he turned his head aside, and in a low tone
which could be heard by all, he said, 'Methinks I can
hear the devil at my elbow saying, 'Knock them down
to me! I will take them.'

Then, after thirty seconds of dead silence, he cried, 'I was going to say, Satan, that you could have them, but' — looking upwards, he said in a loud, clear, yet gentle voice, 'I can hear Jesus saying, "I will take them! I will take them! Unclean, to be washed; drunkards, to be sobered; in all their filth and degradation, I will take them, and cleanse them in mine own blood."

The effects of all this can be better imagined than described. The ministers, preachers and elders were stunned; and the huge congregation was stirred with a spirit of tumultuous joy and exultation.[9]

A man who loves to preach will inevitably love to hear preaching and John Elias was no exception. It was the custom in Wales that at important religious gatherings there would be two preachers. On one such occasion when Jenkin Harry, a well-loved and self-taught minister spoke before Elias, the former delivered a 'perfect specimen of those fervent discourses for which the great Welsh preachers have ever been celebrated.' Apparently when Jenkin Harry ceased, 'John Elias took his place, and, in touching accents, said his predecessor's sermon was so powerful as to overwhelm him. His pent-up feelings were eloquently expressed in a solemn and fervent 'Thank God for the ministry of Jenkin Harry!' That tribute, coming from the greatest Welsh preacher of the day, melted people to tears, and it was only John Elias, and no other, who could have ventured to prolong the service.[10]

Angelsey

In 1799 he moved to Anglesey. Spiritual life on the island just off the Caernafon coast was low at this time. Elias entered

into the work with zeal and enthusiasm and the Lord blessed
his ministry so that 44 chapels were built. He preached for a
whole year on John 17, and also series of sermons from 2
Corinthians 5 and Hebrews 12, and the people flocked to
hear him. Their listening was not a passing curiosity but had a
deep effect upon their lives. Owen Jones says, 'They listened
to him as men that were going to the Judgement Day. The
effects of his preaching were visible and palpable. The owners
of windmills stopped them on the Sabbath day … Drunken-
ness visibly diminished, smuggling was done away with; and
those who had plundered wrecked vessels, took their booty
back again to the seashore. New churches were established,
new chapels built. The gentry of the land, who would never
hear a Dissenter, went gladly to hear John Elias…'[11]

Elias's ministry was based on Anglesey but it covered the
whole of Wales. He gives us a short summary of his travels;

> I travelled much in these years. I went to the South
> (Wales) once every two years, and the alternate year to
> London; besides going to many counties in North
> Wales, and to Liverpool and Manchester, etc. There
> was given to me in those days a fair measure of the
> missionary spirit and a strong desire to speak to the
> most benighted and inconsiderate, — those who would
> not attend a place of worship. In order that such people
> might hear the Word, I preached on the roads, the
> highway, the meadows, etc., in every county in Wales.
> Although the crowds which came to hear were numer-
> ous, and a large number seemed as if they profited by
> hearing, the Lord kept me from being puffed up, — as
> my heart was so corrupt, and the devil so cunning and
> diligent, I trembled many a time lest I should be tempted
> to pride, because of popularity, etc. But the Lord deliv-
> ered me through His grace.[12]

John Elias's life has been summed up as follows;

> It may be said of him, as was said of Moses, that he was faithful in all the house. Faithful as a preacher and pastor, and faithful as a leader and supporter of his denomination; always seen at his post, and in attendance at the meetings of the local church. Presbytery, Associations and other great gatherings. His companionship, sympathy and helpful words were sought after by high and low, poor and rich, and even those who differed from him in matters of politics and religion. To his friends and brother ministers, especially the younger ones, he was most genial, affable and kind, possessing a sweet and pleasant disposition, in conversation unassuming, sincere, and always speaking as becometh a gentleman and a man of God. According to the testimony of friends, neighbours acquaintances and the dearest relatives, his character both at home and abroad was in perfect accord with the truths and graces he preached and recommended to others.[13]

**Please refer to Track 4 of the accompanying CD.
An extract from a sermon preached by John Elias on
Isaiah 49:24.**

References

[1] E. Evans, *John Elias,* Banner of Truth Trust, 1973, p.88.

[2] Evans, *Elias,* pp.89-90.

[3] http://www.christian-bookshop.co.uk/free/biogs/elias.

[4] Ibid.

[5] O. Jones, *Great Preachers of Wales*, Tentmaker, 1885, p. 215.

[6] Evans, *Elias,* pp.258-259.

[7] Evans, *Elias,* pp.354-355.

[8] Evans, *Elias,* p.349.

[9] Evans, *Elias,* pp.143-144.

[10] http://www.red4.co.uk/folklore/trevelyan/glimpse/nonconformists.

[11] Jones, *Great Preachers,* pp.218-219.

[12] Jones, *Great Preachers,* p.2.

[13] http://www.christian-bookshop.co.uk/free/biogs/elias.

5.

J. C. Ryle

John Charles Ryle was born on May 10th 1816. His family were wealthy but more importantly they were Christian. His grandfather had been a personal friend of John Wesley. Ryle became a Christian in 1837,

> Then one Sunday afternoon, he happened to go to a service in one of the parish churches. He remembered nothing particular about it, not even the sermon. But he did respond to the manner in which the second lesson was read — by someone whose name he never knew. The passage was from the second chapter of Ephesians and when the eighth verse was reached, the reader laid emphasis on it with a short pause between each clause. Thus Ryle heard: 'By grace are ye saved — through faith - and that not of yourselves — it is the gift of God.' The same truth which had so transformed Luther in his discovery of justification of faith now had like effect upon Ryle. By the grace of God, he had become a Christian. Henceforth, he would be doughtily upholding Reformation principles.[1]

He said that in 1837 certain truths became very real to him,

> The extreme sinfulness of sin and my own personal
> sinfulness; the entire suitableness of the Lord Jesus
> Christ by His sacrifice, substitution and intercession to
> be the Saviour of the sinner's soul; the absolute neces-
> sity of anybody who would be saved being born again
> or converted by the Holy Ghost; the indispensable ne-
> cessity of holiness of life, being the only evidence of a
> true Christian; the absolute need of coming out from
> the world and being separate from its vain customs, rec-
> reations, and standards of what is right, as well as from
> its sins; the supremacy of the Bible as the only rule of
> what is true in faith or right in practice, and the need of
> regular study and reading it; the absolute necessity of
> daily private prayer and communion with God...[2]

He went on to say, 'People may account for such a change
as they like; my own belief is that no real rational explanation
of it can be given but that of the Bible; it was what the Bible
calls conversion or regeneration. Before that time I was dead
in sins and on the high road to hell, and from that time I have
become alive and had a hope of heaven. And nothing to my
mind can account for it but the free, sovereign grace of God.[3]

As has been mentioned, life was comfortable for the young
Ryle, who as the eldest son of a wealthy landed banker stood
to inherit a large fortune until at the age of twenty-five everything changed; 'it then pleased God to alter my prospects in
life through my father's bankruptcy. We got up one summer's
morning with all the world before us as usual and went to bed
that evening completely and entirely ruined.'[4]

This sad experience shattered the young Ryle. He was so
distraught that he believed he would have committed suicide
if he had not been a Christian. But looking back he could say,

I have not the least doubt it was all for the best. If my father's affairs had prospered and I had never been ruined, my life, of course, would have been a very different one. I should have probably gone into Parliament very soon and it is impossible to say what the effect of this might have been upon my soul. I should have formed different connections, and moved in an entirely different circle. I should never have been a clergyman, never have preached, written a tract or book. Perhaps I might have made shipwreck in spiritual things. So I do not mean to say at all, that I wish it to have been different to what it was. All I mean to say is that I was deeply wounded by my reverses, suffered deeply under them, and I do not think I have recovered in body and soul from the effect of them.[5]

Ryle now had to decide what to do with his life and the result was that he entered the ministry. There seems to be no direct sense of the call of God. Rather, 'I could see nothing before me but to become a clergyman, because that brought me in some income at once.'[6] This does not seem to be a very spiritual reason for entering the Christian ministry, but there can be no doubt that God was using this change of circumstance to direct Ryle in the direction he wanted him to go.

Curate

Ryle began his ministry as a curate at Fawly and Exbury in Hampshire. His rector spent most of his time away in Malta so the new curate had to fend for himself. He said, 'Nobody ever told me what was right or wrong in the pulpit, the result was that the first year of my preaching was a series of experiments.'[7]

Eric Russell tells us that, Ryle soon became accustomed to the routine of pastoral work, carefully preparing two sermons for the Sunday services, regularly conducting meetings twice a week, 'in small crowded cottages, reeking with peat smoke... and was in every house in the parish at least once a month.' His visits were never merely social calls, but always had a spiritual purpose, more so, since his parishioners were 'totally unaccustomed to being ... spoken to about their souls.' At each cottage he left a tract, which he purchased from the Religious Tract Society in Southampton. He stitched brown paper to the covers so that they would last longer and exchanged them between cottagers on his next visit — evangelicals set new standards of pastoral care at this time by their house-to-house visiting, sharing the good news of the gospel, praying with the sick and comforting the dying. In Exbury, the people appreciated Ryle's caring ministry for the two year he was with them and his 'church was soon filled on Sunday.'[8]

Rector

At the age of 27 Ryle became rector of a church in Winchester. He was still inexperienced and said, 'My preaching at Winchester on Sundays consisted entirely of written sermons, of a style I should not care to preach now, because they were far too florid, and far less simple and direct than I afterwards found valuable. Nevertheless, they were thoroughly evangelical and being well-composed and read with a great deal of earnestness and fire. I have no doubt they sounded very fine and effective, but I should not wish to preach them now.[9]

Ryle came to value two prime things in his work in the church — preaching and visiting. His preaching was simple,

as can be seen in his books 'Holiness', and 'Practical Religion'. Clarity and simplicity was his aim. In a chapter entitled
'Simplicity in Preaching', in his book 'The Upper Room', he
made five basic points:

1. have a clear view of the subject upon which you are
   going to preach.
2. try to use in all your sermons, as far as you can,
   simple words.
3. take care to aim at a simple style of composition.
4. use a direct style i.e. using 'I' and 'you' and not 'we.'
5. use plenty of anecdotes and illustrations.[10]

For Ryle, preaching meant exalting Christ, 'If there is no
salvation excepting by Christ we must not be surprised if
ministers of the gospel preach much about him. They cannot
tell us too much about the name which is above every name.
We cannot hear of him too much. We may hear too much
about controversy in sermons, we may hear too much of
works and duties, of forms and ceremonies, of sacraments
and ordinances, but there is one subject which we never hear
too much of, we can never hear too much of Christ.'[11]

He saw the value of pastoral visitation at Exbury and
continued this at Winchester holding that, 'We must talk to
our people when we are out of the church if we would
understand how to preach to them when they are in the
church.'[12] He was in complete agreement with the Scottish
preacher Chalmers who said,'a house-going parson makes a
church-going people.'[13]

A young minister could have no better example than Ryle.
To preach Christ and to exercise a pastoral care over your
people is what the ministry is about. To neglect either is to fail
the people. Pre-eminently they need Christ, but they also

need a pastor who cares for them, has time for them and talks to them.

Ryle was only five months at Winchester before he moved to Helmingham in Suffolk. He was rector there for seventeen years before he moved to Stradbroke in 1861. Eric Russell says, 'Ryle was in his prime at Stradbroke ... It was a great delight to all his parishioners and friends when he announced that he was soon to be married. He had been a widower for less than eighteen months, but he longed for the sustaining companionship of a good Christian woman and a wife who would lovingly mother his family of young children. Ryle's choice of a third wife fell on Henrietta Amelia Clowes, a lady of good birth, highly respected, well educated and a woman with a strong personal faith'.[14]

Bishop

In 1880, totally unexpectedly, and probably more for political rather than spiritual reasons, Ryle was asked by Prime Minister Disraeli to become the first Bishop of Liverpool. He soon discovered the difficulties of being an evangelical Bishop in a broad church. Ryle was never one to compromise on biblical principles but he did feel it was necessary 'to be just and fair and kind to clergymen of every school of thought, whether High or Low or Broad, or of no party.'[15] Inevitably he was criticised by all sides. The Ritualist party regarded him as obnoxious and the evangelicals were unhappy when Ryle consecrated a new church building that was to be used by High Churchmen. They felt that 'the heaviest blow that Protestants have received since the dawn of the Reformation has been inflicted on it by the Bishop of Liverpool.'[16] It is difficult to see how a bishop can please all schools of thought and still be biblical in his actions. The difficulty is perhaps inevitable in a broad church like the Church of England. Clearly, Spurgeon felt the problem when he wrote, 'One of the bravest and best of men is found temporizing in a way which grieves thousands even in his own denomination. Congresses in which Christ and antichrist are brought together cannot but exercise a very unhealthy influence even upon the most decided followers of the truth. We wish Mr Ryle could review his own position in the light of the Scriptures rather than in the darkness of ecclesiasticism; then would he come out from among them, and no more touch the unclean thing.'[17]

Eric Russell sums up Ryle's ministry as follows; 'A hundred years later, we can see that there were few more influential Evangelicals in the Victorian era than Bishop Ryle. though it is a matter of opinion whether he did his best and most lasting work as pastor in Suffolk or as bishop in Liverpool. If the crowning period of his life was the episcopate it was due in part to his strong and robust physique at sixty-four years old, his enormous reserves of energy and his capacity for starting and completing difficult tasks. His capacity for work was astonishing, his use of time was intense, and he was far more active than many younger clergy.'[18]

Books

Ryle was a committed Bible man all his life. He wrote in the preface to Practical Religion,

> After forty years of Bible-reading and praying, meditation and theological study, I find myself clinging more tightly than ever to 'Evangelical' religion, and more than ever satisfied with it. It wears well: it stands the fire. I know no system of religion which is better. In the faith

of it I have lived for the third of a century, and in the
faith of it I hope to die.

The plain truth is, that I see no other ground to occupy,
and find no other rest for the sole of my foot. I lay no
claim to infallibility, and desire to be no man's judge.
But the longer I live and read, the more I am convinced
and persuaded that Evangelical principles are the principles of the Bible, of the Articles and Prayer-book, and
of the leading Divines of the reformed Church of England. Holding these views, I cannot write otherwise than
I have written.[19]

Ryle's 'Expository Thoughts on the Gospels', took him
sixteen years to write and are still published in seven volumes.
They read today as fresh as when they were first written. The
same is true of 'Holiness' and 'Practical Religion', which
ought to be compulsory reading for any evangelical.

**Please refer to Track 5 of the accompanying CD.
Extracts from a sermon preached by J. C. Ryle on
Luke 12:14.**

References

[1] Toon & Smout, *Evangelical Bishop,* Reiner, 1976, p.26.

[2] M. Loane, *Ryle,* Hodder, 1983, p.33.

[3] Loane, *Ryle,* pp.33-4.

[4] D. Holloway, http://www.church.org.uk/resources.

[5] E. Russel, *That Man of Granite,* Christian Focus, 2001, p.32.

[6] Russel, *That Man,* p.35.

[7] Loane, *Ryle,* p.40.

[8] Loane, *Ryle,* p.37.

[9] Russel, *That Man,* p.40.

[10] Holloway, p.7.

[11] Holloway, p.8.

[12] Russel, *That Man,* p.53.

[13] Russel, *That Man,* p.44.

[14] Russel, *That Man,* p.69.

[15] Loane, *Ryle,* p.92.

[16] Loane, Ryle, p.91

[17] I. Murray, *The Forgotton Spurgeon, Banner,* 1966, p.143.

[18] Russel, *That Man,* p.170.

[19] J. C. Ryle, *Practical Religion,* Clarke, 1959, preface.

6.

Robert Murray M'Cheyne

His ministry only lasted seven and a half years and he died at the age of twenty-nine, yet Robert Murray M'Cheyne has had a lasting impact upon Christians for over 150 years. Perhaps the reason for this can be seen in the words of a prayer he often repeated, 'Lord, make me as holy as a pardoned sinner can be.' When a preacher is deeply concerned about personal holiness his ministry will inevitably be enriched to the blessing and profit of the church.

Generally speaking a Christian is as holy as he wants to be. He may say the right words in prayer asking for holiness when in reality he is quite content with a mediocre spiritual life that makes little or no demands upon him. God meets a man at the level of his desires not his words. Those who hunger and thirst after righteousness are given what the soul longs for.

M'Cheyne's prayer for holiness was not words only. He wrote to Horatius Bonar in August 1842, 'I have great desire for personal growth in faith and holiness. I love the Word of God, and find it sweetest nourishment to my soul. Can you help me to study it more successfully? The righteousness of God is all my way to the Father, for I am the chief of sinners; and were it not for the promise of the Comforter, my soul would sink in the hour of temptation.'[1]

He believed that holiness and success were closely linked in a man's ministry as is evidenced by the following: 'but do not forget the culture of the inner man — I mean of the heart. How diligently the cavalry officer keeps his sabre clean and sharp; every stain he rubs off with the greatest care. Remember you are God's sword — his instrument — I trust a chosen vessel unto him to bear his name. In great measure, according to the purity and perfections of the instrument, will be the success. It is not great talents God blesses so much as great likeness to Jesus. A holy minister is an awful weapon in the hand of God.'[2]

Dundee

Robert Murray M'Cheyne was born in Edinburgh in May 1813. He was licensed to preach by the Presbytery of Annan on July 1st 1835, and commenced his ministry at St. Peters, Dundee on November 1st 1836. How does a young man face up to his first pastorate? A man's doctrine will govern both his action and his expectations. He was under no illusions. He saw Dundee as, 'A city given to idolatry and hardness of heart. I fear there is much of what Isaiah speaks of, the prophets prophesy lies, and the people love to have it so.'[3]

M'Cheyne was aware that all his preaching efforts would be in vain if listeners hearts were hard, 'A broken heart alone can receive a crucified Christ. The most, I fear, in all congregations, are sailing easily down the stream into an undone eternity, unconverted ... God help me to speak to you plainly! The longest lifetime is short enough. It is all that is given you to be converted in. In a very little, it will be all over; and all that is here is changing — the very hills are crumbling down — the loveliest face is withering away — the finest garments rot and decay. Every day that passes is bringing you nearer to the judgement-seat...'4

The Bible was the source and totality of M'Cheyne's preaching. He loved God's Word; 'Three chapters of the Word was his usual morning portion. This he thought little enough, for he delighted exceedingly in the Scriptures: they were better to him than thousands of gold or silver. "When you write," said he to a friend, "tell me the meaning of Scriptures." To another, in expressing his value for the Word, he said, "One gem from that ocean is worth all the pebbles of earthly streams."'5

From the outset M'Cheyne's ministry was dominated by his own devotional life before God, his public preaching and also his pastoral visitation. Visiting the sick was clearly important to M'Cheyne as we can see from his notes relayed by Andrew Bonar;

> January 25. 1837 — Visited Mt. M'Bain, a young woman of twenty-four, long ill of decline. Better or worse these ten years past. Spoke of 'The one thing needful, plainly. She sat quiet.
>
> February 14th — Had heard she was better — found her near dying. Spoke plainly and tenderly to her, commending Christ. Used many texts. She put out her hand kindly on leaving.
>
> 15th — Still dying like; spoke as yesterday. She never opened her eyes.
>
> 16th — Shewed her the dreadfulness of wrath; freeness of Christ; the majesty, justice, truth of God. Poor M. is fast going the way whence she shall not return. Many neighbours also always gather in.
>
> 17th — Read Psalm xxii.; shewed the sufferings of Christ; how sufficient an atonement, how feeling a high priest. She breathed loud, and groaned through pain. Died this evening at seven. I hardly ever heard her speak anything;

and I will hope that thou art with Christ in glory, till I go and see.

20th — Prayed at her funeral. Saw her laid in St Peter's churchyard, *the first laid there*, by her own desire, in the fresh mould where never man was laid. May it be a token that she is with Him who was laid in a new tomb.[6]

One of the first things he did at Dundee was to start a weekly prayer meeting in the church. M'Cheyne put a great value on the church meeting together for prayer. He said in a letter, 'No person can be a child of God without living in secret prayer; and no community of Christians can be in a lively condition without unity in prayer.'[7]

In the same letter he goes on to urge Christians to meet regularly, and to pray though what is read in the Bible. 'Pray that you may pray to God, and not for the ears of man. Feel his presence more than man's. Pray for the outpouring of the Spirit on the Church of Christ and for the world — for the purity and unity of God's children — for the raising up of godly ministers, and the blessing of those that are already. Pray for the conversion of your friends, of your neighbours, of the whole town. Pray for the sending of the gospel to the Jews, and to the Gentile nations.

He continues, 'Pride is Satan's wedge for splitting prayer-meetings to pieces — watch and pray against it. If you have not the spirit of God among you, you will have the spirit of the devil. Watch against seeking to be greater than one another; watch against lip-religion. Above all, abide in Christ, and he will abide in you. He is able to keep you from falling, and to make you happy, holy young men.'[8]

M'Cheyne preached at St. Peters to a congregation of over a 1,000 each Sunday and said, 'the reason why some of the worst sinners in Dundee had come to hear him, was because his heart exhibited so much likeness to them.' A more probable explanation as suggested by Andrew Bonar is that, 'There is a wide difference between preaching *doctrine* and preaching *Christ*. Mr M'Cheyne preached all the doctrines of Scripture as understood by our Confession of Faith, dwelling upon ruin by the Fall, and recovery by the Mediator ... it was not *doctrine* alone that he preached; it was *Christ*, from whom all doctrine shoots forth as rays from a centre. He sought to hang *every* vessel and flagon upon him.'[9] When Christ is exalted he draws men to himself.

All the time M'Cheyne was at Dundee his health was poor. Some thought he ought to move to a country church which would better suit his poor health. But his conviction of being placed by God in Dundee never wavered — 'My Master has placed me here with his own hand and I never will, directly or indirectly, seek to be removed.'[10]

He would not move church but his health deteriorated so much towards the end of 1838 that his doctors insisted he stop working. He therefore returned to his parents in Edinburgh to rest.[11]

It was not until November 1839 that his health allowed him to return to St. Peters. During his absence W. C. Burns was standing in for him and under his ministry Dundee experienced remarkable blessing. Murray says, 'When M'Cheyne, restored to health, returned to St. Peter's in November of that year, he viewed an unforgettable scene. A deep concern and impression of eternal realities possessed the vast congregation. In worship "the people felt that they were praising a present God."' Such a sight as this was not uncommon throughout the remainder of his ministry. The grief at sin which filled the hearts of many could only be expressed by tears; the distress expressed by one awakened sinner to M'Cheyne represented the feeling of scores — 'I think,' he said, 'hell would be some relief from an angry God...' The Word was listened to on these occasions with 'an awful and breathless stillness.'[12]

His legacy

Robert Murray M'Cheyne was not alive long enough to become an old, wise, experienced minister. He was always a young man yet he demonstrated a holiness of life and closeness to God that must be the greatest legacy that any man can leave in this world. Holiness has nothing to do with age or maturity. It stems from the longing of the heart of a believer for his God. M'Cheyne had this longing in abundance,

> I am ... deepened in my conviction, that if we are to be instruments in such a work, we must be purified from all filthiness of the flesh and spirit. Oh, cry for personal holiness, constant nearness to God, by the blood of the Lamb. Bask in his beams — lie back in the arms of love — be filled with His spirit — or all success in the ministry will only be to your own everlasting confusion.
> You know how I have always insisted on this with you. It is because I feel the need thereof myself. Take heed, dear friend; do not think any sin trivial; remember it will have everlasting consequences...How much more useful might we be, if we were only more free from pride, self-conceit, personal vanity, or some secret sin that our heart knows. Oh! hateful sins, that destroy our peace and ruin souls![13]

It would have been easy for M'Cheyne to be rather envious of the blessing attending Burns preaching at St. Peters during his absence. But the opposite was true. He wrote to Burns in November 1839,

> You may believe that it was with a thankful, joyful spirit that we read of these things. I cannot rest till I hear from you what has been done among my own dear flock. I do not like to impose a task on you; but if you have an

hour's leisure, it would be truly gratifying to me to hear
from you, before I come over, a minute account of all
that God seems to have wrought in Dundee during my
absence. You remember it was the prayer of my heart
when we parted, that you might be a thousand fold more
blessed to the people than ever my ministry had been.
How it will gladden my heart, if you can really tell me that
it has been so. My poor, dear flock, hard-hearted and
stiff-necked as they were, if the Lord has really opened
their hearts, and brought them to a saving knowledge of
Christ, and if their hearts and lives are together changed, I
will bless God while I have any being.[14]

Every day of such a short ministry is to be treasured and it
may be difficult to understand why the Lord curtailed even
those few years with so much illness. But M'Cheyne had no
problem understanding this, 'When I was laid aside from the
ministry, I felt it was to teach me the need of prayer for my
people. I used often to say, Now God is teaching me the use of
prayer. I thought I would never forget the lesson, yet I fear I *am*
grown slack again when in the midst of my work.'[15]

M'Cheyne clearly knew the importance of prayer for success
as a preacher and in his daily walk with his Lord. Just a few
months before his death he said, 'I ought to spend the best
hours of the day in communion with God. It is my noblest and
most fruitful employment.'[16]

A young preacher can glean much wisdom from the writings
and thoughts of a man like M'Cheyne. He once advised, for
example, 'Study holiness of life. Your whole usefulness depends
on this, for your sermons last but an hour or two; your life
preaches all the week.' On another occasion he wrote, 'A man
cannot be a faithful minister, until he preaches Christ for Christ's
sake — until he gives up striving to attract people to himself and
seeks only to attract them to Christ.'[17]

By any standard Robert Murray M'Cheyne was a remarkable man. Indeed David Smithers sums up his life by saying, 'It was not Robert Murray M'Cheyne the people saw, it was Jesus'.[18] He made a difference to the lives he touched in his ministry, and he still does today. His life should cause any young preacher to want a ministry that counts. An older man may well ask, 'what have I done with the many years God gave me to preach?' For any preacher M'Cheyne is a challenge and a reminder that 'a holy minister is an awesome weapon in the hand of God'.[19]

Please refer to Track 6 of the accompanying CD. Extracts from a sermon preached by Robert Murray M'Cheyne at St Peter's Church, Dundee in February 1837 on John 16:8.

References

---

[1] A. Bonar, *Memoirs & Remains,* William Middleton, 1846, p.274.

[2] Bonar, *Memoirs,* p.243.

[3] Bonar. *Memoirs,* p.57.

[4] I. Murray, Banner of Truth Trust Article, Nov 2001, p.3.

[5] Bonar, *Memoirs,* p.55.

[6] Bonar, *Memoirs,* p.58.

[7] Bonar, *Memoirs,* p.236.

[8] Bonar, *Memoirs,* pp.237-8.

[9] A. Bonar, *The Life of Robert Murray M'Cheyne,* Banner of Truth Trust, 1972, p.78.

[10] A. Bonar, *M'Cheyne,* p.81.

[11] Murray, pp.4-5.

[12] Murray, p.6.

[13] Murray p.6.

[14] Bonar, *Memoirs,* p.234.

[15] Bonar, *Memoirs,* p.242.

[16] D. Smithers, *Robert Murray M'Cheyne,* http://www.watchword.org/smithers, 2003.

[17] Smithers, *Robert Murray M'Cheyne.*

[18] Smithers, *Robert Murray M'Cheyne.*

[19] Smithers, *Robert Murray M'Cheyne.*

7.

Charles Spurgeon

'Young man,' said the preacher, addressing one member of his small congregation, 'you look very miserable, and you will always be miserable if you do not obey my text.' The fifteen-year-old boy could have been offended by such a personal application from the pulpit, but he was not. On many occasions he had heard better preachers and better sermons, but never had he heard God speaking to him as on that never to be forgotten morning in Colchester. It seemed that all his young life he had been searching for a real and deep experience of God. His background and upbringing could have led him to assume that he was a Christian, but his heart told him it was not so. The Bible, which he knew well, confirmed that he had to be born again. But how and when? The answer came in the most unexpected place, from the most unexpected human source, but unmistakably it was God saying to him, 'Look unto me and be ye saved.'

The young man was Charles Haddon Spurgeon and the date was 6 January 1850. He was fifteen years old. By the age of seventeen he was pastor of Waterbeach Baptist Church, and at nineteen he was called to the pastorate of New Park Street

Chapel in London. This is an amazing story and breaks all the rules for the need of experience and maturity in ministers. Which church today would call a teenager to be its pastor? But Spurgeon was no ordinary teenager and there have been few, if any preachers, like him before or since.

To understand this man we need to understand his doctrine. He was a Baptist and a Calvinist.

Baptist

Spurgeon's father and grandfather were congregational ministers so his believers baptism convictions were not inherited. In fact, his father was not too keen to see his son baptised. On 6 April 1850 he wrote to his father,

> My dear father, You will be pleased to hear that, last Thursday night, I was admitted as a member. Oh, that I may henceforth live more for the glory of him by whom I feel assured that I shall be everlastingly saved! Owing to my scruples on account of baptism, I did not sit down at the Lord's table, and cannot in conscience do so until I am baptised. To one who does not see the necessity of baptism, it is perfectly right and proper to partake of this blessed privilege; but were I to do so, I conceive would be to tumble over the wall, since I feel persuaded it is Christ's appointed way of professing him. I am sure this is the only view which I have of baptism. I detest the idea that I can do a single thing towards my own salvation. I trust that I feel sufficiently the corruption of my heart to know that, instead of doing one iota to forward my own salvation, my own corrupt heart would impede it, were it not that my Redeemer is mighty, and works as he pleases.[1]

He concluded the letter,

As Mr Cantlow's baptising season will come round this month, I have humbly to beg your consent, as I will not act against your will, and should very much like to commune next month. I have no doubt of your permission. We are all one in Christ; forms and ceremonies, I trust, will not make us divided.

His father was slow in answering, and so Charles with his usual impatience wrote to his mother on 20 April:

My dear mother, I have every morning looked for a letter from father. I long for an answer; it is now a month since I have had one from him. Do, if you please, send me either permission or refusal to be baptised; I have been kept in painful suspense. This is the 20th, and Mr Cantlow' s baptising day is…next week. I should be sorry to lose another ordinance Sunday; and with my present convictions I shall never so violate my conscience as to sit down unbaptised.[2]

The longed-for letter arrived on 25 April, but it was not altogether to Charles' liking. He wrote in his diary for that day, 'A letter from father: in truth, he is rather hard upon me.' It appears that John Spurgeon did not refuse his son permission to be baptised, but he expressed certain fears. Charles refers to these in the entry in his diary for the following day: 'How my father's fears that I should trust to baptism stir up my soul! My God, thou knowest that I hate such a thought.'[3] Obviously, he was very upset by his father's letter, but permission was granted.

His soul was not stirred up for too long, and on another occasion he was able to joke with his mother on the subject: 'My mother said to me, one day, "Ah, Charles! I often prayed to the Lord to make you a Christian, but I never asked that you might become a Baptist." I could not resist the temptation to reply, "Ah, mother! the Lord has answered your prayer with his usual bounty, and given exceedingly abundantly above what you asked or thought."'[4]

It was no small thing for a fifteen-year-old to take such a stand. He recounts for us his feelings at the time:

> I had attended the house of God with my father, and my grandfather, but I thought, when I read the Scriptures, that it was my business to judge for myself. I knew that my father and my grandfather took little children in their arms, put a few drops of water on their faces, and said they were baptised. But I could not see anything in my Bible about babes being baptised. I learned a little Greek, but I could not discover that the word 'baptise' meant to sprinkle, so I said to myself, 'They are good men, yet they may be wrong; and though I love and revere them, that is no reason why I should imitate them.' And they acknowledged, when they knew of my honest conviction, that it was quite right for me to act according to my conscience. I consider the 'baptism' of an unconscious infant is just as foolish as the 'baptism' of a ship or a bell, for there is as much Scripture for the one as for the other. Therefore, I left my relations, and became what I am today, a Baptist, so called, but I hope a great deal more a Christian than a Baptist.[5]

Calvinist

Spurgeon never did have any formal theological training, but he was none the poorer for this. It was quite normal for him to live and think in the realm of theological truths and doctrines. Early in his life, his heart and mind embraced the great biblical truths that history has called Calvinism.

He said, 'It is a great thing to begin the Christian life by believing good solid doctrine. Some people have received twenty different "gospels" in as many years; how many more they will accept before they get to their journey's end, it would be difficult to predict. I thank God that he early taught me the gospel, and I have been so perfectly satisfied with it that I do not want to know any other. Constant change of creed is sure loss. If a tree is to be taken up two or three times a year, you will not need to build a very large loft in which to store the apples. When people are always shifting their doctrinal principles, they are not likely to bring forth much fruit to the glory of God. It is good for young believers to begin with a firm hold upon those great fundamental doctrines which the Lord has taught in his Word. Why, if I believed what some preach about the temporary, trumpery salvation which only lasts for a time I would scarcely be at all grateful for it; but when I know that those whom God saves he saves with an everlasting salvation, when I know that he gives them an everlasting righteousness, when I know that he settles them on an everlasting foundation of everlasting love, and that he will bring them to his everlasting kingdom, oh, then I wonder, and I am astonished that such a blessing as this should ever have been given to me!'[6]

Calvinism to Spurgeon was only another way of describing the biblical theology of the Lord Jesus Christ and the apostle Paul. He said, 'We use the term then, not because we impute any extraordinary importance to Calvin's having taught these doctrines. We should be just as willing to call them by any other name, if we could find one which would be better understood … I have my own private opinion that there is no such thing as preaching Christ and him crucified, unless we preach what nowadays is called Calvinism … I do not believe we can preach the gospel if we do not preach justification by faith, without works, nor unless we preach the sovereignty of God in his dispensation of grace; nor unless we exalt the electing, un-changeable, eternal, immutable, conquering love of Jehovah; nor do I think we can preach the gospel, unless we base it upon the special and particular redemption of his elect and chosen people which Christ wrought out upon the cross, nor can I comprehend a gospel which lets saints fall away after they have been called, and suffers the children of God to be burned in the fires of damnation after having once believed in Jesus. Such a gospel I abhor!'[7]

The whole of Spurgeon's preaching obviously flowed out of this doctrine. The sovereignty of God was the key to everything, and truths like election, perseverance and particular redemption were not to be apologised for but proclaimed with passion and authority.

New Park Street

The congregation at New Park Street was in decline when Spurgeon arrived. It was, in his own words, 'a mere handful of people'. Actually, there were 200 who worshipped there regularly. By today's standards that would be a strong church, but in 1854 it was a mere handful. Obviously, to the new pastor it was a small church, but he was in no doubt that these believers had a great spiritual strength. They were a praying people. They knew how to plead with God. 'We had prayer meetings in New Park Street that moved our very souls. Every man seemed like a crusader besieging the New Jerusalem, each one appeared determined to storm the Celestial City by the might of intercession, and soon the blessing came upon us in such abundance that we had not room to receive it.'[8]

The combination of the preaching gifts of Spurgeon and the prayers of the church was mighty in the hand of God. The congregation multiplied rapidly and soon the twelve hundred seats were all full Sunday after Sunday. The spiritual blessing created physical problems. A packed building, with gas lights burning, was not the most comfortable place, particularly as the windows were not made to open, Charles urged the deacons to do something about the lack of air. On several occasions he asked them to remove the upper panes of glass, but nothing was done. In the end he solved the problem himself with the aid of his walking stick! The chapel building was only just over twenty years old and the deacons seemed reluctant to do any structural alterations to accommodate the growing congregation. In sheer frustration Spurgeon was moved one night in the middle of a sermon to declare, 'By faith the walls of Jericho fell down, and by faith, this wall at the back shall come down too.' After the service one of the older and more prudent deacons rebuked him with the words: 'Let us never hear of that again.' Spurgeon replied, 'You will hear no more about it when it is done, and therefore the sooner you set about it the better.'9

The pastor had his way, and at a church meeting on 30 August 1854, the following resolution was passed: 'That we desire, as a church, to record our devout and grateful acknowledgements to our heavenly Father for the success that has attended the ministry of our esteemed pastor and we consider it important, at as early a period as possible, that increased accommodation should be provided for the numbers that flock to the chapel on the Lord's days...'10

Success is always a dangerous thing to handle. This is particularly true for a young man. Pride and arrogance can often follow rapidly on the heels of success with devastating effects. When such amazing success came to the nineteen-year-old Spurgeon he was spared the problems of pride. In fact his reaction was quite the opposite; his success frightened him, 'I hope I was not faithless, but I was timorous, and filled with a sense of my own unfitness ... I felt myself a mere child.'11

God's hand was obviously upon this young pastor. He was spared the awful spiritual paralysis of pride and given a wisdom that was far beyond his years. A new pastor inevitably has to face problems inherited from the previous ministry. Spurgeon was no exception, but his approach to the situation was a prudent one that young ministers would do well to imitate, 'I am quite certain that, for my own success, and for the prosperity of the church, I took the wisest course by applying my blind eye to all disputes which dated previously to my advent. It is the extremity of unwisdom for a young man, fresh from college, or from another charge, to suffer himself to be earwigged by a clique, and to be bribed by kindness and flattery to become a partisan, and so to ruin himself with one-half of his people.'12

Opposition

The impact of Spurgeon's preaching upon London was amazing. By the beginning of 1855 the chapel in New Park Street was too small to accommodate the crowds attending and urgent work began on enlarging the building. In the meanwhile, the services were held in the Exeter Hall. Such success was not good news to everyone concerned with the religious life of London, and soon the young preacher was the target of a vicious series of articles and letters in the public press. The writers were mainly ministers and church people.

The Rev. Charles Banks wrote in the *Earthen Vessel* December 1854, 'Mr C. H. Spurgeon is the present pastor of New Park Street Chapel, in the borough of Southwark. He is a young man of a very considerable ministerial talent, and his labours have been amazingly successful in raising up the drooping cause at Park Street to a state of prosperity almost unequalled. We know of no Baptist minister in all the metropolis — with the exception of our highly-favoured and long-tried brother, James Wells, of the Surrey Tabernacle — who had such crowded auditories, and continued overflowing congregations, as Mr Spurgeon has. But then, very solemn questions arise: What is he doing? Whose servant is he? What proof does he give that, instrumentally, his is a heart-searching, a Christ-exalting, a truth-unfolding, a sinner-converting, a church-feeding, a soul-saving ministry?'[13]

This was mild compared with the following month's edition of the same publication. A long letter bearing the signature 'Job' (Spurgeon believed the writer was the James Wells referred to above) contained the following, 'Mr Spurgeon was, so says the *Vessel*, brought to know the Lord when he was only fifteen years old. Heaven grant it may prove to be so — for the young man's sake, and for that of others also! But I have — most solemnly have — my doubts as to the divine reality of his conversion. I do not say — it is not for me to say — that he is not a regenerated man, but this I do know, that there are conversions which are not of God.' After making that most serious charge as to Spurgeon's conversion, the writer dismissed his ministry by asserting that it was 'most awfully deceptive', and that he 'is simply deceiving others with the deception wherewith he deceives himself.[14]

Many other letters, for and against, followed. The *Ipswich Express* of February 1855 included a letter with a particular accusation: 'Actually, I hear, the other Sunday, the gifted divine had the impudence, before preaching, to say, as there were many young ladies present, that he was engaged — that his heart it was another's, he wished them clearly to understand that — that he might have no presents sent him, no attentions paid him, no worsted slippers worked for him by the young ladies present. I suppose the dear divine has been rendered uncomfortable by the fondness of his female auditors; at any rate, such is the impression he wishes to leave.'[15]

Such attacks upon a very young and inexperienced
minister were amazing. He felt deeply these slanders but he
had the wisdom to see beyond the petty jealousies of men.'[16]
Spurgeon was one of a long line of gospel preachers who had
suffered in the same way. He was neither the first nor the last to
have to face the slanders and lies of outraged religious men.
Perhaps we can best understand these attacks by referring to a
letter in the *Essex Standard* of April 1855 from a supporter of
Spurgeon. He wrote,

> The pulpit is now too much abused by the mere display
> of intellect; instead of the indignant burst of a Luther
> against the iniquities of mankind, we have only the pas-
> sive disapprobation of the silvery-tongued man of let-
> ters. The preachers address their cold, "packed-in-ice"
> discourses to the educated portion of their audience;
> and the majority, the uneducated poor, are unable, in
> these "scientific" sermons, to learn the way of holiness,
> from the simple fact that they are above their compre-
> hension.
> Mr Spurgeon goes to the root of the evil; his discourses
> are such as a child can understand, and yet filled with the
> most elevating philosophy and sound religious instruc-
> tion. Taking the Word as his only guide, and casting
> aside the writings — however antiquated — of fallible
> men, he appeals to the heart, not to the head; puts the
> living truth forcibly before the mind, gains the attention,
> and then, as he himself says, fastens in the bow the
> messenger shaft, which, by the blessing and direction of
> the Almighty, strikes home to the heart of the sinner.[17]

To many of Spurgeon's contemporaries he was an Arminian. One reason for this wrong assessment was that *every*
week sinners were being saved through his preaching. Men and

women were making open profession of faith in response to his ministry. To many Calvinists who saw little of this in their churches this had to mean that the one preaching to them was an Arminian.

The Calvinist always presents a more biblical gospel to the sinner than the Arminian, but when it comes to reaping what has been sown some Calvinists flounder and get confused. In many ways they are afraid to reap. They are so afraid to attribute to the sinner any ability to save himself, that this fear causes them in their preaching to take away the sinners responsibility to seek a way out of sin.

It is true that the sinner has no ability to save himself but it is not true that he has no responsibility. When the gospel tells men and women to repent, to come to Jesus, it is telling them that they have this responsibility. When the sinner sees this and tries to come to Christ he will discover he cannot do it. He is then thrown back on the grace and mercy of God for his salvation.

Spurgeon preached to men and women in such a way that caused them to seek the Lord with great urgency. This in turn caused them to depend entirely upon grace to save them. Spurgeon showed them the way of salvation as well as telling them of their sin and guilt. God blessed this and thousands of sinners came to saving faith. The critics of Spurgeon failed to see that the problem was not in Spurgeon's preaching but in theirs.

This was not true of all the critics. James Wells was severe in his attacks upon Spurgeon but he was a great preacher who had built up a congregation of over 2000 at the Surrey tabernacle.

It is often said that there is no such thing as bad publicity. This certainly proved true at New Park Street. The stories of Spurgeon in the press brought many curious listeners to the church. This became so marked that Spurgeon noted that

'Great numbers of the converts of those early days came as a direct result of the slanders with which I was so mercilessly assailed.'[18]

Preaching

Charles Spurgeon was known as the Prince of Preachers. His preaching was Bible based and Christ-centred, and marked by a great passion to see souls saved. He believed that 'soul-winning is the chief business of the Christian minister.'[19] But he knew that 'we have before us a mighty work, for which we are of ourselves totally incapable. No minister living can save a soul; nor can all of us together, nor all the saints on earth or in heaven, work regeneration in a single person. The whole business on our part is the height of absurdity unless we regard ourselves as used by the Holy Ghost, and filled with His power.'[20]

This conviction did not cause him to lose sight of the preacher's responsibility in bringing the gospel to sinners. He knew the heart of man, and said, 'A sinner has a heart as well as a head; a sinner has emotions as well as thoughts; and we must appeal to both. A sinner will never be converted until his emotions are stirred. Unless he feels sorrow for sin, and unless he has some measure of joy in the reception of the Word, you cannot have much hope of him...Religion without emotion is religion without life.'[21]

For this reason sermons should not be boring. 'That is what you must do with your sermons, make them red-hot; never mind if men do say you are too enthusiastic, or even too fanatical, give them red hot shot, there is nothing else half as good for the purpose you have in view. We do not go snow-balling on Sundays, we go fire-balling; we ought to hurl gre-nades into the enemies ranks.'[22]

Coupled with this, sermons should be clear and uncompli-
cated. 'If the people are to be saved, it must be by *sermons that
interest them*. You have first to get them to come under the
sound of the gospel, for there is, at all events in London, a great
aversion to a place of worship, and I am not much surprised
that it is so concerning many churches and chapels. I think, in
many instances, the common people do not attend such
services because they do not understand the theological "lingo"
that is used in the pulpit; it is neither English, nor Greek, but
Double-dutch... No, brethren, we must preach in what Whitefield used to call "market language" if we would have all classes
of the community listening to our message.'[23]

Preaching for Spurgeon was never simply an exercise in
communication but involved passion and urgency; 'You must
have, more or less, a distinct sense of the dreadful wrath of God
and of the terrors of the judgement to come, or you will lack
energy in your work, and so lack one of the essentials of
success. I do not think the preacher ever speaks well upon such
topics until he feels them pressing upon him as a personal
burden from the Lord.'[24]

The Down Grade Controversy

It caused Spurgeon deep distress to see inroads being made
into the Baptist Union of doctrines that were not biblical. He
saw the implication of this as disastrous, writing in 1889,
'Attendance at places of worship is declining, and reverence for
holy things is vanishing; and we solemnly believe this to be
largely attributable to the scepticism which has flashed from the
pulpit and spread among the people ... Have these advanced
thinkers filled their own chapels? Have they, after all, prospered
through discarding the old methods? ... It now becomes a
serious question how far those who abide by the faith once

delivered to the saints should fraternise with those who have turned aside to another gospel. Christian love has its claims, and divisions are to be shunned as grievous evils; but how far are we justified in being in confederacy with those who are departing from the truth?'[25]

According to Michael Haykin, 'As Spurgeon had examined the preaching of some of his Baptist contemporaries, he had noticed in their sermons that the "Atonement is scouted, the inspiration of Scripture is derided, the Holy Spirit is degraded into an influence, the punishment of sin is turned into fiction, and the resurrection into a myth." He felt that he could no longer remain in alliance with those proclaiming such views and thus had no option but to lead the Metropolitan Tabernacle out of the Baptist Union.[26]

It was at the annual meeting of the Union in April 1888 that the final split came. Iain Murray says, 'for Spurgeon, far from being a basis for reunion it but confirmed him in his conviction that his resignation must be irrevocable'.[27] His comments in *The Sword and the Trowel* for June tell us his feelings, 'I am not, however, careful to criticise the action of a body from which I am now finally divided. My course has been made clear by what has been done. I was afraid from the beginning that the reform of the Baptist Union was hopeless, and therefore I resigned. I am far more sure of it now, and should never under any probable circumstances dream of returning.'[28]

The fight for the truth cost Spurgeon greatly. Others knew he was right but kept silent. But it was not in the nature of the man to be silent when the gospel was 'being buried beneath the boiling mud-showers of modern heresy'. He said, 'I am quite willing to be eaten by dogs for the next fifty years but the more distant future shall vindicate me!'[29]

Charles Haddon Spurgeon died in Mentone, in the south of France, on 31 January 1892, and thus ended one of the most remarkable ministries England has known. Countless thousands were brought to Christ through his preaching and during his pastorate in London 14,691 were received into membership.

Please refer to Track 7 of the accompanying CD. Extracts from a sermon preached by Charles Spurgeon on October 2nd, 1859 on Hebrews 13:20.

References

[1] C. H. Spurgeon, *The Early Years,* Banner of Truth Trust, 1976, p.116.

[2] Spurgeon, *Early Years,* p.116.

[3] Spurgeon, *Early Years,* pp.129-130.

[4] Spurgeon, *Early Years,* p.45.

[5] Spurgeon, *Early Years,* p.145.

[6] Spurgeon, *Early Years,* p.163.

[7] Spurgeon, *Early Years,* p.168.

[8] Spurgeon, *Early Years,* p.263.

[9] Spurgeon, *Early Years,* p.271.

[10] Spurgeon, *Early Years,* p.271.

[11] Spurgeon, *Early Years,* p.264.

[12] Spurgeon, *Early Years,* p.265.

[13] Spurgeon, *Early Years,* p.305.

[14] Spurgeon, *Early Years,* p.307.

[15] Spurgeon, *Early Years,* p.311.

[16] Spurgeon, *Early Years,* p.312.

[17] Spurgeon, *Early Years,* p.318.

[18] Spurgeon, *Early Years,* p.329.

[19] C. H. Spurgeon, *The Soul Winner,* Pilgrim, 1978, p.11.

[20] Spurgeon, *Soul Winner,* p.27.

[21] Spurgeon, *Soul Winner,* p.22.

[22] Spurgeon, *Soul Winner,* pp.75-76.

[23] Spurgeon, *Soul Winner,* pp.95-96.

[24] Spurgeon, *Soul Winner* pp.162-3.

[25] I. Murray, *The Forgotten Spurgeon,* Banner of Truth Trust, 1966, p.149.

[26] C. H. Spurgeon, *The Saint & his Saviour,* Evangelical Press, 2001, p.21.

[27] Murray, *Forgotten Spurgeon,* pp.154-5.

[28] Murray, *Forgotten Spurgeon,* p.155.

[29] Murray, *Forgotten Spurgeon,* p.22.

8.

A. W. Tozer

Aiden Wilson Tozer was born on a farm in Pennsylvania in 1897. He never liked his first names and preferred to be called by the initials A W, or just Tozer. He became a Christian in 1917. He had little formal education and no theological training. His doctorate was honorary. But he had a great desire to preach and very soon after his conversion was an active street preacher. He held a few short pastorates and in 1928 went to Southside Alliance Church in Chicago where he remained until 1959. There his ministry blossomed. David Fant says, 'The church was generous in sharing their pastor's ministry with others, and from coast to coast he became known as a speaker at missionary conventions, Bible conferences, and meetings of clergymen. To relieve him of the necessity of visitation the church provided assistants. The fact that he seldom called on anyone gave rise to a story which is perhaps apocryphal. One of his elders was sick, and Tozer, chancing to be in the neighbourhood, decided to drop by. The elder, looking toward the door and seeing Tozer, exclaimed: "Dear Lord! I'm not that sick, am I?"'[1]

For a man with little education his reading appetite was wide. He read theology, history, philosophy and poetry. He loved the ancient writers especially the Church Fathers and Christian mystics. But above all he gave top priority to the Bible. Fant says, 'With dictionary, lexicon, and concordance at hand he sought the etymology of all doubtful words; and long hours were devoted to memorising the Scriptures and great poets. The accuracy and appropriateness of his quotations in sermons and writings reflected his familiarity with many branches of learning; he seemed always to have at hand what he wanted when he wanted it. When his sons were in college they often marvelled at their father's acquaintance with their subjects. Scholastic attainments were recognised in the granting to him of an honorary Doctor of Letters degree by Wheaton College in 1950 and a Doctor of Law degree in 1952 by Houghton College.'[2]

Preaching

Tozer took preaching very seriously and had no patience with gimmicks of any kind. He said, 'A preacher not long ago announced that he would have for his subject the next Sunday evening, "Don't Tear Your Shirt." He took for his text these words, "Rend your hearts and not your garments," and preached on repentance. It is that kind of thing that makes atheists. To approach a solemn subject in such a flippant manner is inexcusable. It is time the Christian public goes on a gracious and dignified strike against such comic-strip parody of gospel preaching.'[3]

This did not mean that his sermons were heavy. On the contrary he believed that, 'A church can wither as surely under the ministry of soulless Bible exposition as it can where no Bible at all is given. To be effective the preacher's message must be alive; it must alarm, arouse, challenge. It must be God's present voice to a particular people. Then, and not till then, is it the prophetic word and the man himself a prophet.'[4]

Tozer did not court popularity and was not afraid to stand alone. He once said that he had preached himself off every major Bible conference in the country. Warren Wiersbe tells us that 'The entire focus of Dr. A. W. Tozer's preaching and writing was on God. He had no time for religious hucksters who were inventing new ways to promote their wares and inflate their statistics. Like Thoreau, whom he read and admired, Tozer marched to a different drummer; and for this reason, he was usually out of step with many of the people in the religious parade.'[5]

James Snider is clear as to the main thrust of Tozer's ministry,

> Primarily, A. W. Tozer was a preacher. All else revolved around his pulpit ministry. His writing, for example, was simply an extension of his preaching...
>
> During the 1930s and 40s, Tozer's preaching gained attention in the Chicago area because it was different. While others were offering clever outlines and meticulous word studies, Tozer led his listeners straight into the presence of God. That was his goal, his objective in preaching.
>
> Tozer studiously avoided any artificiality in his preaching. Alliteration he regarded as in that category and avoided it. Anything that might distract from the core message or block his hearers' path to God was ruthlessly cut out. His sermons were warm and alive ... He worked hard not to sound like a typical preacher.[6]

Snider continues, 'Tozer's sermons were never shallow. There was hard thinking behind them, and Tozer forced his hearers to think with him. He had the ability to make his listeners face themselves in the light of what God was saying to them. The flippant did not like Tozer; the serious who wanted to know what God was saying to them loved him. Often his messages were so strong — and long — some wished he would stop and let them catch their breath.'[7]

Many of Tozer's sermons are available on tape for us today.[8] No one could claim that they could not understand the preaching. They may not like the straight talk of Tozer but they certainly know what he is saying. He was not a dynamic preacher, more homespun, but people listened to him because they recognised that he listened to God. He confronted people with God and left the Christian with no excuse for a worldly lifestyle.

Books

Tozer wrote only nine books but many more have been compiled from his sermons and magazine editorials. Like his sermons, the books put their finger on the shallowness of evangelical life in the 20th century. Dr. Lloyd-Jones in recommending *The Pursuit of God*, wrote, 'Any book that stimulates and increases ones hunger and thirst for God is invaluable. This book does that in a most profound manner. I would say that of all contemporary writers Dr. Tozer probes the soul, exposes all shame, and leads to the heights of true spiritual worship in an incomparable manner. I am happy to recommend it. I shall never forget my first reading of it. May this book be widely read and pondered.'[9]

In his *The Old Cross and the New,* Tozer makes a devastating assessment of much of modern evangelicalism. The following is a long quote but worth reading as it clearly shows Tozer's great burden for the state of the modern church:

> All unannounced and mostly undetected there has come in modern times a new cross into popular evangelical circles. It is like the old cross, but different: the likenesses are superficial; the differences, fundamental...The old cross would have no truck with the world. For Adam's proud flesh it meant the end of the journey. It carried into effect the sentence imposed by the law of Sinai. The new cross is not opposed to the human race; rather, it is a friendly pal and, if understood aright it is the source of oceans of good clean fun and innocent enjoyment. It lets Adam live without interference. His life motivation is unchanged; he still lives for his own pleasure, only now he takes delight in to sing choruses and watching religious movies instead of singing bawdy songs and drinking hard liquor. The accent is still on enjoyment, though the fun is now on a higher plane morally if not intellectually...
>
> The new cross does not slay the sinner, it redirects him. It gears him into a cleaner and jollier way of living and saves his self-respect. To the self-assertive it says, 'Come and assert yourself for Christ.' To the egotist it says, 'Come and do your boasting in the Lord.' To the thrillseeker it says, 'Come and enjoy the thrill of Christian fellowship.' The Christian message is slanted in the direction of the current vogue in order to make it acceptable to the public.
>
> The philosophy back of this kind of thing may be sincere but its sincerity does not save it from being false. It is false because it is blind. It misses completely the whole meaning of the cross.
>
> The old cross is a symbol of death. It stands for the abrupt, violent end of a human being. The man in Ro-

man times who took up his cross and started down the road had already said good-by to his friends. He was not coming back. He was going out to have it ended. The cross made no compromise, modified nothing, spared nothing; it slew all of the man, completely and for good. It did not try to keep on good terms with its victim. It struck cruel and hard, and when it had finished its work, the man was no more...

We who preach the gospel must not think of ourselves as public relations agents sent to establish good will between Christ and the world. We must not imagine ourselves commissioned to make Christ acceptable to big business, the press, the world of sports or modern education. We are not diplomats but prophets, and our message is not a compromise but an ultimatum.

God offers life, but not an improved old life. The life He offers is life out of death. It stands always on the far side of the cross. Whoever would possess it must pass under the rod. He must repudiate himself and concur in God's just sentence against him.

What does this mean to the individual, the condemned man who would find life in Christ Jesus? How can this theology be translated into life? Simply, he must repent and believe. He must forsake his sins and then go on to forsake himself. Let him cover nothing, defend nothing, excuse nothing. Let him not seek to make terms with God, but let him bow his head before the stroke of God's stern displeasure and acknowledge himself worthy to die.[10]

When Tozer looked at the church he was not impressed. He said, 'Our trouble is not that we refuse to believe right doctrine, but that we refuse to practise it.'[11] Evangelicalism he believed was in a rut and rut leads to rot: 'The church is afflicted by dry rot. This is best explained when the psychology of nonexpectation takes over and spiritual rigidity sets in, which is an inability to visualise anything better, a lack of desire for improvement.'[12]

Tozer was convinced that the main threat to the modern church is routine, or rather when routine becomes 'lord' in church life,

> When we come to the place where everything can be predicted and nobody expects anything unusual from God, we are in a rut. The routine dictates and we can tell not only what will happen next Sunday, but what will occur next month and, if things do not improve, what will take place next year. Then we have reached the place where what has been, determines what is, and what is, determines what will be.
> That would be perfectly all right and proper for a cemetery. Nobody expects a cemetery to do anything but conform... But the church is not a cemetery and we should expect much from it because what has been should not be lord to tell us what is, and what is should not be ruler to tell us what will be. God's people are supposed to grow.[13]

Tozer does probe the soul but his message is not negative. All the time he seeks to point us to the greatness and majesty of God. His advice to Christians is to listen to God,

> When you introduce God, a new thing happens. 'I will make a way in the wilderness.' Who ever heard of it? 'I will make rivers in the desert.' Who ever heard of it? Unbelief is logical and true to nature because nature is fixed in a regular routine. You may expect nature to continue to go right on in that routine. However, another factor is

now introduced. God introduces the supernatural, and He says, 'I am who I am and I will.' God wills to do a new thing.

We keep going the way of nature in the fixed routine. You cannot expect anybody to do anything about it. But I hear another voice saying, 'I am who I am.' Since I have been a Christian, I have lived for that voice. I have lived to hear God say, 'I am who I am you can't but I can. You aren't, but I am. You are not able, but I am able. You have no wisdom, but I am Jehovah and I have the wisdom.'

We approach Him through Jesus Christ His Son. Never forget that all the power of this great Jehovah with His awful and awesome glorious names is channelled through the person of His Son, Jesus Christ, to His people. Jesus dug a channel, so to speak, through to the mighty ocean that is Jehovah so all the sweet waters, the healing waters, the soul-quenching waters that are God can flow down to the Lord's people if they would only believe.[14]

Please note — as a wealth of Tozer's recorded material is available from good Christian bookshops, an extract has not been placed on the accompanying CD.

References

[1] D. Fant, *A. W. Tozer*, Christian Publications,1964, p.20.

[2] Fant, *Tozer*, p.22.

[3] J. Snyder, *In Pursuit of God,* Christian Publications, 1991, p.79.

[4] Snyder, *In Pursuit,* p.79.

[5] Snyder, *In Pursuit,* p.84.

[6] Snyder, *In Pursuit,* p.103.

[7] Snyder, *In Pursuit,* p.107.

[8] Anchor Recordings Ltd, 72 The Street, Ashford, Kent.

[9] M. Lloyd-Jones, *The Pursuit of God,* Marshall, Morgan & Scott, 1961, Fly cover.

[10] A. W. Tozer, *Man the Dwelling Place of God,* Christian Publications. 1966, p.42.

[11] A. W. Tozer, *Out of the Rut into Revival,* Hodder, 1992, p.121.

[12] Tozer, *Out of the Rut,* p.8.

[13] Tozer, *Out of the Rut,* pp.5-6.

[14] Tozer, *Out of the Rut,* p.160.

9.

Martyn Lloyd-Jones

Martyn Lloyd-Jones died on March 1, 1981 at the age of 81. The April issue of Evangelical Times began its report on his funeral with these words, 'Friday is market day in Newcastle Emlyn, a small country town nestling in the beautiful Teifi valley about ten miles from the old county town of Cardigan. But on Friday March 6 about 1,000 people came to Newcastle Emlyn not to buy or sell cattle, but for an entirely different purpose. They came from all parts of the British Isles to join in the funeral service for Dr. Martyn Lloyd Jones.'

If it were possible they would have come from all parts of the world. I was in Australia when I heard that the Doctor had died. I was having lunch with a young pastor from New Zealand who had never met Lloyd-Jones but had read his books. He said, 'I feel as though I have lost a friend.' Clearly Dr. Lloyd-Jones made a difference to the lives of countless numbers of Christians world-wide. The reason for this is beautifully explained in the words of a fourteen year old boy who was asked to prepare a short talk for his English lesson at school on 'the most interesting person I have ever met.'

He chose as his subject Dr. Lloyd-Jones and said, 'When Dr. Lloyd-Jones came to our home, he was very kind and understanding. When talking to him, I felt there was no gap between us (as I feel there is between me and most people who are as old as he is!) He didn't talk down to me. Although he was such a great man, he had time to talk to us children. He listened to us, and at the meal table we had lots of fun. He was gentle and yet strong... I'm so sorry I shall never meet him or hear him preach again. This country has certainly lost the most interesting man I ever met.'[1]

It was this characteristic that made the Doctor a pastor to the pastors, and many men going into the ministry in the 1960s and 70s could testify to the great help he was to them. In 1971 I was having serious problems in my church that looked as if they could end my ministry. In desperation I decided to 'phone the Doctor for his advice. I had been at many conferences when he was the speaker, but I had never spoken personally to him, so I was rather apprehensive. When he answered the 'phone, I explained who I was and that I had a church problem I would like to speak to him about. To my amazement, he said he knew who I was and knew all about my problem. He went on to say that in a few weeks time he would be preaching on a Tuesday at the Heath church in Cardiff and would see me following the meeting. He gave me an hour of his time and his advice and concern were a great encouragement to me. I am sure that many other ministers could say the same thing.

Sandfields

Dr. Lloyd-Jones undertook his medical training at Barts, one of the great teaching hospitals in London. He became chief clinical assistant to Sir Thomas Horder who was doctor to King Edward VII. By the age of twenty six Lloyd-Jones, writes Fred Catherwood, 'was well on the rungs of the Harley Street ladder, with a brilliant and lucrative career in front of him. Then something happened'.[2]

He had always been religious and was a member of the church, but, says Iain Murray, 'Dr Lloyd-Jones came to see that his outward life had been little more than play-acting: the real truth was that he had been seeking to escape from God. This knowledge did not come to him in days, nor even weeks. He put no date to his conversion.'[3]

With his conversion came a great desire to preach the gospel and in 1927 he and his wife Bethan, left London to take up the pastorate of one of the Presbyterian Forward Movement halls in the poor district of Sandfields, Aberavon. Gwyn Williams, one of the Doctor's successors in the pulpit at Sandfields tells us,

> Immediately he came, the congregation grew. At first the motive was curiosity, but soon people came under the influence of the preaching and were converted... In one eighteen month period there was exceptional unction on the ministry, and the attendance was such that the chapel became too small to hold the crowd,
>
> So an annexe was added to the chapel building...
>
> There were many conversions. Some who were already members of the church made a profession, confessing their faith before the congregation. Others from quite a different background turned to Christ — among them tramps, drunkards and boxers. It was the custom, when people made a profession, to receive them into membership immediately, but if they did not give evidence of perseverance in their new-found faith, they could as swiftly be removed from the church register.
>
> One remarkable conversion was that of the church secretary. Although it was he who had first felt the urge to invite the Doctor to Sandfields, he was not a believer. In-

deed, socialist politics were his life, and he had every prospect of a brilliant future. But he too came under the influence of the preaching and believed. The result was that he put aside his politics completely — an event which caused a real stir in the area! — and threw himself increasingly into the work of the church and the gospel.[4]

The eleven years at Sandfields were remarkable for the impact made by the ministry. There were two reasons for this. One was the witness of the Doctor's life and concern for the people. At the end of the Sandfields ministry a reporter for a national English newspaper wrote this,

> For eleven years now Dr Martin Lloyd-Jones has been a minister in Aberavon, and around him has grown a living legend of sainthood.
>
> I came through dull streets to learn something of this legend — the legend which you will never learn from the 'beloved doctor' himself. Hundreds of humble dwellers in Aberavon, church members or not, regard Martyn Lloyd-Jones, the man to whom all men are brothers as a matter of course, with a reverent gratitude that holds a touch of awe.
>
> There are a thousand splendid deeds of Aberavon's doctor-saint over the past eleven years, that will never, perhaps, be told, yet, in their cumulative influence, they seem to sweeten this little town even as the strong winds from the Severn sweeten and cleanse it. He has spent, they say, a small fortune in giving practical help to people in need of money, has helped them to clear off arrears of rent and even to buy their homes. His constant question at meetings of his church committee is: 'Now, who is there in real want?'

Here in Aberavon they pray he will come back to them. When I asked why he had decided to leave Aberavon and the little wind-swept church, a friend told me: 'I do not know. I only know that he has decided nothing in his life — not the slightest thing — except after many hours of prayer.'[5]

The other reason was the preaching. Another reporter wrote in his paper,

> Mine was a human failing of curiosity on visiting the Bethlehem Forward Movement Church, Aberavon, last Sunday. Curiosity soon vanished, however. The presence of the young doctor in the pulpit. the tremendous zeal revealed in his preaching, the air of great faith and certainty that he carried, all combined to sweep it away. I remained to wonder and to respect.
> I do not crave the reader's pardon for abandoning my usual manner of writing my impressions and for giving to the best of my ability, as much of the sermons as possible. I do this simply because the sermons in themselves were stirring, because Dr Lloyd-Jones has something to say, and because they are the words of one who has felt himself forced to speak by a greater than human power. My versions of the sermons are but a weak picture of the originals, but I dare to hope that the reader will get a faint conception of the tremendous impetus behind the preacher.[6]

Iain Murray says of this report, 'Sam Jones seems to have been one of the first to recognise in print that what was most unusual about the young preacher was not his change of career but his message itself and the manner in which it was delivered. Thus he closed his column with the question; 'Has the future

marked him down as a great leader of the nation? Of this I am
certain, if ever a man was called to the ministry it is Dr Martyn
Lloyd-Jones.'[7]

Dr. James Packer heard Lloyd-Jones preach in the late
1940s and wrote, 'I had never heard such preaching and was
electrified. All that I know about preaching, I can honestly say, I
learnt from the Doctor. I have never heard another preacher
with so much of God about him.'[8]

Lloyd-Jones was first and foremost a preacher. Very many
books have appeared under his name but most of them are
sermons he had already preached. He was a preacher and
thought of himself primarily as an evangelist. It was his conviction that one of the two Sunday sermons should always be
evangelistic. At a ministers' conference where he had voiced his
views on mass evangelism, in the discussion one minister asked
him aggressively, 'When did you last have an evangelistic
campaign in your church.' Coolly and calmly, the Doctor
answered, 'Every Sunday evening.'

Hundreds were converted at Sandfields and when I took up
the pastorate there in 1986, forty seven years after he had left,
there were still about thirty people there who had been saved
under the Doctor's ministry. Obviously they were elderly by
then, but they all spoke with immense gratitude to the power of
the preaching they had heard in their youth.

Westminster Chapel

Lloyd-Jones began his ministry at Westminster Chapel in
September 1939 and remained there until 1968. Concerning
this move from South Wales Elwyn Davies wrote, 'As is so often
said on such occasions, 'Wales's loss was surely England's
gain.' However influential his ministry might have been in
Wales, 'how can one begin to compute the influence for good

of this prince among preachers, this wise counsellor and spiritual leader, through his pulpit ministry, his Friday evening lectures, his meetings for ministers, the Westminster Conferences, his wider preaching ministry, his availability at all times for counsel and advice — a ministry which is to continue through his printed works and through the kind providence that has enabled his spoken word to be preserved, so that to an uncanny degree we are able to hear the Doctor as though he were yet with us? All these things, we now know, hinged upon his ministry at Westminster Chapel. We can only say with the Apostle, 'How unsearchable are his judgements, and his ways past finding out!' (Romans 11:33)

It proved to be Wales' gain also, despite the fact that after the 1939-45 war, when it was evident that Nonconformity was losing its grip on the people, Dr. Lloyd-Jones would occasionally be criticised for forsaking Wales in its hour of need. However, he never lost touch with the situation in Wales, nor did he ever show any sign of rancour or bitterness as a result of what had happened. He continued to preach to vast congregations in many centres in Wales. In 1977, for example, he celebrated his fiftieth consecutive annual visit to preach at Carmarthen.'[9]

The days of the Second World War (1939-1945) were difficult ones to be a minister in London. The congregation at Westminster Chapel shrunk to less than 200, but by 1947 the average morning congregation was 1500 and the evening 2000. The preaching these folk heard was outstanding. Graham Harrison says,

> What he did was to send you away with a renewed conviction of the greatness and the glory of the gospel, of the power of the living God, and of his love to us in sending his dear Son Christ Jesus to die for us sinners on Calvary's hill So humbling! But so uplifting and exhilarating.

It was not that he was always the same. In fact you could
say that he cultivated three distinct styles. There were the
Friday evenings at Westminster as he worked his way
through the riches of the mightiest of all the Epistles. As
he used to say, that was 'more cerebral'. Sunday morning
was a ministry largely with the saints in mind — heart-
warming, encouraging, inciting to the knowledge and experience of God. Then on a Sunday evening he would
blow the gospel trumpet with an authority and in a style
that were unmatched.

The same variations could be seen as he made his weekly
ventures through the length and breadth of the British
Isles ... I number some of the most thrilling moments of
my life in such meetings. What a great gospel! What a
glorious Saviour![10]

The Doctor used to say that he would not cross the road to hear
himself preach, but many would not agree with him on this. We
were on holiday in the Lake District and heard it announced at
the morning service we attended that Dr. Lloyd-Jones was to
preach that evening in a barn on a farm in Cumberland. It took
us hours to find that barn but the journey was worth it to hear
such powerful preaching. Lloyd-Jones's preaching made his
listeners think and very often challenged views that had been
held dearly for years. Leith Samuel says, 'I can still visualise the
spot where I sat in Westminster Chapel while the Doctor
expounded the doctrine of election. I had been brought up to
believe that because God knows everything He knows which
way we are going to jump by the exercise of our own free-will.
And here was the Doctor demolishing that idea for all he was
worth. I boiled with indignation! Gradually I saw my problem
was not with the Doctor and his apparently new interpretation,
but with the very words of John 17. Did I really believe Scripture was the Word of God? Indeed I did. Then I must submit

my mind to all its truth and abandon my ill-thought-out ideas. I must acknowledge I was a Christian because God had chosen me in Christ before the foundation of the world. This didn't mean I was no longer responsible for my actions. I must exercise the renewed will He had given me, freely and intelligently, for His glory and according to His Word. But it did mean that *all* the credit for my salvation could and would go to a gracious and loving God who had laid hold of me long before I dreamed of laying hold of Him. My indignation was replaced with gratitude for the Doctor's merciless logic.'[11]

Controversies

Not everyone held Lloyd-Jones in high regard and his stance on some issues involved him in controversy. He was one of the few evangelicals who did not support the Billy Graham Campaign at Haringey in 1954. In an interview Carl Henry asked him, 'what specific reservations do you have about modern evangelicalism as such?' Lloyd-Jones answered,

I am unhappy about organised evangelism and even more about the invitation system of calling people forward … Mark you, I consider Billy Graham an utterly honest, sincere, and genuine man … He, in fact, asked me in 1963 to be chairman of the first Congress on Evangelism, then projected for Rome, not Berlin. I said I'd make a bargain: if he would stop the general sponsorship of his campaigns — stop having liberals and Roman Catholics on the platform — and drop the invitation system, I would wholeheartedly support him and chair the congress. We talked for about three hours, but he didn't accept these conditions.

I just can't subscribe to the idea that either congresses or campaigns really deal with the situation. The facts, I feel, substantiate my point of view: in spite of all that has been done in the last 20 or 25 years, the spiritual situation has deteriorated rather than improved. I am convinced that nothing can avail but churches and ministers on their knees in total dependence on God. As long as you go on organising, people will not fall on their knees and implore God to come and heal them. It seems to me that the campaign approach trusts ultimately in techniques rather than in the power of the Spirit. Graham certainly preaches the Gospel. I would never criticise him on that score. What I have criticised, for example, is that in the Glasgow campaign he had John Sutherland Bonnell address the ministers' meetings. I challenged that. Graham replied, 'You know, I have more fellowship with John Sutherland Bonnell than with many evangelical ministers.' I replied, 'Now it may be that Bonnell is a nicer chap than Lloyd-Jones — I'll not argue that. But real fellowship is something else: I can genuinely fellowship only with someone who holds the same basic truths that I do.'[12]

Herbert Carson wrote,

To contend is one thing; to be contentious is another and the latter he tried to avoid... His primary call was to preach the Word, to call sinners to Christ, to lead Christians to holy living, to promote spiritual growth and unity in the churches. His ultimate vision was the vindication of the gospel, the honour of Christ and the glory of God. To reach these goals he spared no effort and shirked no contest, even if it meant misrepresentation by his critics, and misunderstanding by his friends.

Of course, he made mistakes... he was impatient at times, for with his own brilliant clarity of mind he found it hard to suffer fools gladly... but beyond all his weaknesses it he was like Bunyan's 'Mr. Valiant-for-truth'. He forced generations of young ministers to think clearly about the great issues of Scripture. He exposed the shallowness, the inconsistency and the confusion of their previous positions. He enthused them with a love for God and for God's truth. Above all he showed them that it is not simply Christ in the head who is the goal of our endeavours, but Christ dwelling in our hearts, and reigning as Lord in his church.[13]

In October 1966 The Doctor was invited to speak on Christian Unity at the Second National Assembly of Evangelicals. Graham Harrison wrote of that meeting,

He was attempting to get evangelicals to face up to the doctrine of the Church ... They were always afraid that someone would be offended and that divisions would be caused. Often, so he argued, 'evangelicals ... seem more concerned to maintain the integrity of their denominations than anyone else in the denominations associated with evangelical work in London. They were always afraid that someone would be offended...
The argument was biblical, the reasoning sound and the delivery moving. But, as the Doctor had always feared, so far as the majority of evangelicals were concerned, it fell on deaf ears. The Evangelical Alliance had sponsored the meeting and had invited Dr. Lloyd-Jones to speak to this subject and to repeat in public the arguments he had previously put in private to their Commission on Church Unity. In the light of this, the congregation were amazed when the chairman — Anglican John R. W. Stott — took

the surprising step of virtually rebuking the speaker and declaring that history ... and Scripture was against him, in that the remnant was within the Church and not outside it.[14]

Later John Stott wrote,

In his view of the church he was a strong independent, and could not understand how any Evangelical remained a member of a 'mixed denomination' like the Church of England. For years he continued to argue that consistent evangelicals should secede. At the National Assembly of Evangelicals in the Central Hall, Westminster, in October 1966 he issued a stirring appeal to us to come out and form a faithful evangelical 'remnant.' I was in the chair and, when he had finished his address, felt it right to disassociate myself from his position. I did so in the hope of dissuading some ministers from writing precipitate letters of resignation before the matter had been discussed (as it was to be) in the following days. But later I called on Dr Lloyd-Jones to apologise — not for what I had said (which I still believe) but for misusing the chair and almost turning the meeting as he put it) into a 'debate.' He told me that he had scarcely restrained himself from answering me and developing the debate.

But we continued to have a warm personal relationship. I always had a strong affection and admiration for him. In an era of theological flux he stood firm for historic, biblical Christianity. And although he was a polemical speaker, he always distinguished between principles and personalities, and was at heart a man of love and peace. 'The Doctor' was a spiritual father figure to many of us. His death has created a serious vacuum.[15]

Christ — the first and the last

The opening and closing sentences of Dr Lloyd-Jones' last sermon at Sandfields, Aberavon, on the fiftieth anniversary of his settlement in that congregation, February 6, 1977.

There are two reasons for this text [1 Cor 2:2] tonight, the first being that it was this text which was laid upon my heart, when I first preached in Sandfields, at the evening service of Nov 28th, 1926. The second reason is, that this text describes exactly the commission given to any true preacher of the Gospel. It also delineates the basic factor which should be controlling every Christian life. Paul 'determined not to know anything among you, save Jesus Christ, and him crucified'. He could have decided otherwise, and in so doing, no doubt, he would have soon won the acclaim of the Greeks, by preaching to them their own brand of wisdom. But no! He deliberately became a fool in their eyes. He became a fool for Christ's sake, preaching to them a Gospel which he realised would be foolishness to the Greeks, and to the Jews a stumbling block. This, I say, was a deliberate decision on Paul's part.

Why did he come to this decision? I say it in all humility. Why did I come to the same decision 50 years ago in this building? — and why have I done so again tonight ? Why should all true preachers of the Gospel, and all true churches, come to the same conclusion as Paul? I firmly believe that a refusal to do so is a direct cause of the Church's witness to the world being so equivocal, of her preachers, in so many parts, being so ineffectual — so weak and helpless in standing against the forces of evil...

Is Christ everything to you? Is He central to your life? Nothing else works, either for you as individuals, or for us as a nation. All things change — we have seen many changes over 50 years. Many who came to see that the Gospel actually works 50 years ago are now in the Glory. We must all face death — all else must come to nought. What will you have when your end draws near? I tell you now with all the earnestness at my command, apart from Christ you will have *nothing*. Only Jesus Christ and Him crucified can avail — only He can make you a new man, a new woman. You can become a saint. In Christ you will be able to join with those we knew here 50 years ago who have now left this world and are basking in the sunshine of His face.[16]

Please note — as a wealth of Lloyd-Jones' recorded material is available from good Christian bookshops, an extract has not been placed on the accompanying CD.

References

[1] Evangelical Times, April 1981, p.9.

[2] Evangelical Times, April 1981, p.8.

[3] I. Murray, *The First 40 Years,* Banner of Truth Trust, 1982, p.64.

[4] G. Williams, EMW magazine, April 1981, pp.14-15

[5] Murray, The First 40 Years, p.340.

[6] Murray, The First 40 Years, p.144.

[7] Murray, The First 40 Years, p.146.

[8] J. Packer commendation on Lloyd Jones, 'The Expository Sermons on 2 Peter', Banner of Truth Trust, 1983, fly cover.

[9] E. Davies, EMW magazine, April 1981, p.25.

[10] G. Harrison, Evangelical Times, April 1981, p.12.

[11] F. Catherwood, *Chosen by God,* Highland, 1986, p.197.

[12] M. Lloyd-Jones, *Chosen,* pp.100-101.

[13] Herbert Carsen, Evangelical Times, p.15.

[14] Harrison, EMW, pp.40-41

[15] J. Stott, *Chosen,* p.207.

[16] Banner of Trust Trust magazine, May 1981, pp.32-33.